D1461747

Joseph Ward's memoirs will open up an a̶̶ ̶̶ ̶̶ ̶̶ ̶ ̶̶ ̶̶ ̶̶ ̶̶ ̶̶ ̶ ̶̶ ̶̶ ̶̶ ̶̶ ̶̶ ̶̶ ̶ ̶̶ ̶̶ ̶̶ and family history which is not well documented. The migrant story is commonly and understandably one of deprivation: that of. the landless Catholics. Joe Ward's story varies the pattern. The story is fascinating. As human history, as economic history, as Irish history, it deserves to be told.

Dr Brenda Niall, author and Fellow of the Australian
Academy of the Humanities

Joe Ward's memoirs give us a worm's-eye view, a sense of the lived experience of a class of people that has remained hitherto obscure. Artfully arranged and edited in this book, they have a vivid life of their own. Critics and artists will find that the book gives an immediate access to the mental world in which so much of the classic period of Irish modernity unfolds. Both for its immediacy and its long-term impact, this is an important book.

Fintan O'Toole

Joe Ward's simple, austere yet entertaining storytelling style captures the mood and drama of the cattle fairs of the late-nineteenth and early-twentieth century. Joe has a memory for detail, not just for his own experiences, but also for those of his father and even his grandfather. Ciaran Buckley preserves Joe Ward's storytelling style, his turn of phrase and his worldview. Overall, this is an engaging and well-written book which will be of particular interest to those seeking an insight to life in rural Ireland from another era.

James Morrissey, author of 'On the Verge of Want'
and 'A History of the Fastnet Lighthouse'

While primarily a historical document, *Strong Farmer* has the readability and effect of a creative piece. I am intrigued by all sorts of details, some of them asides, others extended; the kinds of hotel for instance where the traders in cattle stayed in distant towns for a fair day, what they ate . . . . The narrator is interesting in himself. And through him, vacancies in the picture of rural life at a certain period are filled in.

Anne Haverty

First published in 2007 by
Liberties Press
Guinness Enterprise Centre | Taylor's Lane | Dublin 8 | Ireland
www.LibertiesPress.com
+353 (1) 415 1224 | info@libertiespress.com

Distributed in the United States by
Dufour Editions
PO Box 7 | Chester Springs | Pennsylvania | 19425

and in Australia by
James Bennett Pty Limited | InBooks
3 Narabang Way | Belrose NSW 2085

Trade enquiries to CMD Distribution
55A Spruce Avenue | Stillorgan Industrial Park | Blackrock | County Dublin
Tel: +353 (1) 294 2560 | Fax: +353 (1) 294 2564

Copyright © Ciaran Buckley and Chris Ward, 2007

The authors have asserted their moral rights.

ISBN: 978–1–905483–24–2

2 4 6 8 10 9 7 5 3 1

A CIP record for this title is available from the British Library

Map by Ciara Foster
Illustrations by Michael Shannon
Set in Garamond
Printed in Ireland by Colour Books | Baldoyle Industrial Estate | Dublin 13

Liberties Press gratefully acknowledges the financial assistance of the Arts Council in
relation to the publication of this title.

This book is sold subject to the condition that it shall not, by way of trade or
otherwise, be lent, resold, hired out or otherwise circulated, without the
publisher's prior consent, in any form other than that in which it is published and
without a similar condition including this condition being imposed
on the subsequent publisher.
No part of this publication may be reproduced or transmitted in any form or by
any means, electronic or mechanical, including photocopying, recording or storage in
any information or retrieval system, without the prior permission
of the publisher in writing.

STRONG FARMER

THE MEMOIRS OF JOE WARD

CIARAN BUCKLEY
AND CHRIS WARD

To my sister Olivia, with thanks for all her help over the years – CW

Contents

Map by Ciara Foster

6

RAIL ROUTES FOR THE LIVE EXPORT TRADE

WARD   MAC an BHAIRD

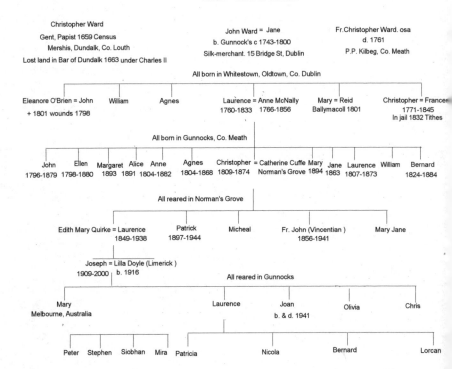

Christopher Ward
Gent, Papist 1659 Census
Mershis, Dundalk, Co. Louth
Lost land in Bar of Dundalk 1663 under Charles II

John Ward = Jane
b. Gunnock's c 1743-1800
Silk-merchant. 15 Bridge St, Dublin

Fr.Christopher Ward. osa
d. 1761
P.P. Kilbeg, Co. Meath

All born in Whitestown, Oldtown, Co. Dublin

Eleanore O'Brien = John   William   Agnes   Laurence = Anne McNally   Mary = Reid   Christopher = Frances
+ 1801 wounds 1798   1760-1833   1766-1856   Ballymacoll 1801   1771-1845
                                                                                                            In jail 1832 Tithes

All born in Gunnocks, Co. Meath

John   Ellen   Margaret   Alice   Anne   Agnes   Christopher = Catherine Cuffe   Mary   Jane   Laurence   William   Bernard
1796-1879 1798-1880   1893   1891 1804-1882 1804-1868   1809-1874   Norman's Grove   1894   1863   1807-1873   1824-1884

All reared in Norman's Grove

Edith Mary Quirke = Laurence   Patrick   Micheal   Fr. John (Vincentian)   Mary Jane
                    1849-1938   1897-1944   1856-1941

Joseph = Lilla Doyle (Limerick)
1909-2000   b. 1916

All reared in Gunnocks

Mary   Laurence   Joan   Olivia   Chris
Melbourne, Australia   b. & d. 1941

Peter   Stephen   Siobhan   Mira   Patricia   Nicola   Bernard   Lorcan

WARD FAMILY TREE

Preface

The Writing of *Strong Farmer*

This book came about as a result of a conversation that I had with Chris Ward in the autumn of 2005. I had written an article for a local-history publication on the pivotal role that 'strong farmers' and the cattle trade played in Irish political and economic affairs between the end of the Napoleonic Wars and the early 1960s. The specifics of the article were based on information I had from my mother's family, who – like Joe Ward and his predecessors – had bought cattle in the fairs in the west and the south, finished them in County Meath, and sold them in the Dublin cattle market for export to England and Scotland.

When Chris mentioned that she had spent almost twenty years recording her father's stories about the cattle trade, I immediately knew that she had captured something both important and unique. Joe was the only child of a man who was born only a few years after the Famine. Joe was his father's closest companion for many years, which is why his stories reach so far back into the nineteenth century.

Joe was also a natural storyteller, so my main task – as a writer and as an editor – was to let Joe tell his own story. As far as possible, the stories are presented in Joe's words, in his style, and using the facts as he presented them. However, the anecdotes have been sorted into themes and placed in chronological order.

I've added a number of sections in italics, to place Joe's stories in a historical context. These sections are as sparse and factual as possible, to avoid distracting from Joe's narrative. The textbooks that I found most useful were *The Course of Irish History* by T. W. Moody and F. X. Martin; *Ireland Since the Famine* by F. S. L. Lyons; and *Modern Ireland* by Mark Tierney. The more specialised reference books included *The Modernisation of Irish Society* by Joseph Lee; *Atlas of the Irish Rural Landscape* by Aalen, Whelan and Stout; *Land, Politics and Nationalism* by Philip Bull; and *The*

Blueshirts and Irish Politics by Mike Cronin. I have also drawn on *Ríocht na Midhe*, the historical periodical that covers topics relevant to County Meath and Westmeath, particularly an article entitled 'Local Government and Local Power in Meath, 1925–1942', which was written by Thomas M. Wilson.

The various legal and family documents that have been placed throughout this book were also provided by Chris Ward, without whom this book could never have been written.

I would like to thank my children Matthew and Elizabeth, who tolerated my absences in the evenings and on weekends; my wife Therese for her support and encouragement; Seán O'Keeffe and Peter O'Connell of Liberties Press for taking on new authors with obscure subject matter, and Orlaith Delaney for her work on the text; the Arts Council for their financial support; Ciara Foster for her map of Irish cattle trade routes; Helen Sheehy for her legal advice; Fintan O'Toole, Anne Haverty, James Morrissey and Brenda Niall for their encouragement; Áine McCarthy, David Miller, Ross Kerber, Maura Conron, Maureen Howard and Donald Faulkner for persuading me that non-fiction is the most powerful way to tell a story; and for my brothers, sister and parents, who have reminded me on many occasions that I ought to write a book.

Ciaran Buckley

My thanks to Ned Byrne, St Vincent's Hospital; Dr Anne O'Dowd; Peter Haldun; Brian Donnelly NAI; my sister Mary for her historical knowledge; and Olivia for her suggestions and information.

Chris Ward

FOREWORD

The world presented in this book was in headlong decline by the late 1960s and early 1970s. A combination of factors – including Ireland's accession into the European Common Market, the urbanisation and modernisation of Irish society, and the industrialisation of the Irish agricultural industry – swept away the factors that allowed the cattle industry to be a dominating influence in the social and economic life of Ireland.

On the one hand, it is fascinating to relive that world through this book. On the other hand, it is interesting to see that some factors in that world are still with us today. We should not forget that, even in the final years of the 1980s, the politics and economics of the live cattle export trade remained contentious, not only between farmers and non-farmers, but also between different groups of farmers.

This account is a vivid history of a particular aspect of Irish farming. Although the 'Strong Farmers' were mostly associated with specific parts of Counties Meath and Dublin, they had an influence on farming in Connacht and Munster, as well as on sections of the working class and the middle class in the city of Dublin and in market towns all over the country.

The book is strongest on the details of the farming economy in Ireland from the introduction of the Corn Laws at the end of the eighteenth century until the middle of the twentieth century. Farming practice, both in tillage and in livestock rearing, lies at the heart of this memoir. The level and detail of knowledge is impressive. Joe describes the art of stacking unthreshed corn on platforms, which rested on granite pillars to avoid infestation by mice. He even describes the drinking habits of any mouse fortunate enough to find its way into a stack – and links this to the misfortunes of families who did not pay attention to the tiny but important methods of good farming practice.

It is a shock to be reminded that the plains of Royal Meath – where, in living memory, ploughing was regarded as a mortal sin – once produced abundant crops of wheat and oats. Equally, the modern farmer and meat processor would be appalled at the idea of long-horned twelve-hundredweight bullocks and eleven-hundredweight heifers, both of which were much prized in the early twentieth century.

The reader is drawn into the varied – and usually unpleasant – business of lodging in poor flea-ridden accommodation and arguing about the 'luck penny' in provincial fairs. The book describes the roughnecks at the fairs; the cheats, drunks and fighters; the jockeying for position in the Dublin cattle market; the competition for places in the cattle wagons; and the arrangements to secure payment before leaving for home.

Today's livestock farmers can bring stock to the mart and be home in time for tea and the six-one news. Nevertheless, the mart is still the occasion for networking, the exchange of practical experience, and the forging of expressions of sectoral interests.

The historical sections threaded through the text give a succinct and direct account of the political background to the memoir. The brief description of the circumstances of de Valera's decision to launch the Economic War against the UK is particularly striking. It gives a bare-bones account of the clash between fundamentalist republicanism and irredentist imperialism. In contrast, Joe's words give an eloquent, if rather laconic, account of how ordinary people suffered from a clash which most of them did not understand.

This is folk memory at its very best, at its most evocative, and at its most pungent. Every family should have a history told like this; every parish should have a multitude of them. Such memoirs are an invaluable aid to understanding and making sense of our history and of the social, cultural and political strands of which it is woven.

Alan Dukes
4 June 2007

INTRODUCTION

My name is Joe Ward, from Gunnocks, Clonee, in County Meath. I have been asked to put down my recollections of the last two generations of the Ward family and the people who worked with them. I am very pleased to do this and hope my account may be of some interest.

I have no qualifications for writing other than a good memory. I will write these articles the same way as I talk: short, factual and to the point. Most of the events of which I will speak took place before the year I was born, 1909.

I know that some people will say 'What a pity he did not say what happened to so-and-so' or 'What did the landlord do then?' The answer is that I do not know. I have done very little research into the family history, other than the information I obtained from members of the older generation or from old account books.

The Ward family came to Gunnocks from Whitestown, near Oldtown in County Dublin, around 1700. The family had lived at Whitestown for hundreds of years and a branch of the family is living there still.

The Wards lived in Whitestown beside the home of Molly Weston, the woman who led the United Irishmen at the Battle of Tara in 1798. At the end of the nineteenth century there were four boys and two girls in the family. The eldest was John, who inherited Whitestown; the second was Laurence, who inherited Gunnocks from a relative who had moved to Dublin to be a silk merchant in Bridgefoot Street; another brother, Christopher, moved to Fieldstown in County Dublin. Norman's Grove is a short distance from Gunnocks, as is Nuttstown. All the farms mentioned are between Dunboyne, Clonee, Kilbride and Ratoath. Fieldstown and Whitestown are a number of miles away in north County Dublin, between Rolestown and Swords.

Because of their historic connection to County Dublin, the Wards looked to County Dublin for most things, such as wives, workmen and a place to be buried. In 1845, three of the families of workmen were from County Dublin. The Phoenix family came from Donabate; the Rodgers family came from Saucerstown, near Swords; and the Geraghty family came from Greenogue.

The Wards were hard-working people, in the sense that they looked after their business very well. They were a very shrewd business family and they did not mix in politics. They looked after the people in the locality and were looked up to by all of the local people. I suppose this was because of their straightforwardness and their interest in the things of the parish and the local people.

I do not know the meaning of the word 'Gunnocks', which has been spelled many different ways down through the centuries. In 1520, it was spelled 'Cannocke'. In 1560, it was spelled 'Conock'. In 1736, it was spelled 'Gunnocks' and 'Gunog'.

According to P. W. Joyce's *Place Names*, it means 'sandy hill', or 'the place of the sand'. Those readers who can speak Irish will understand how Joyce comes to this conclusion. However, this locality is not known for sand any more than any other part of south Meath.

Another possibility is that the word has French origins, since the Plunkett family came from Normandy in France originally and may have retained some French words, even as late as the seventeenth century.

When a person writes a history or a book, it is usual at the end of the book to thank the people who gave help to the writer. In my case, I prefer to mention those people to whom I am indebted for information at the beginning.

My father – Laurence Ward – was born in Norman's Grove in 1849 and died in 1938 at the age of eighty-eight. My cousin – Laurence Ward of Fieldstown East – died unmarried at the age of eighty-six, shortly after the end of the Second World War. His sister – Sarah Ward of Fieldstown East – died unmarried at the age of ninety-three in 1954. I wish to say that the minds and memories of the three old people above were perfect up to the moment of their deaths. I would also like to thank my wife Lilla, who memorised much of what Sarah told her and has looked up some old books and papers for me. I would also like to thank my daughter Chris, who did decades of research.

Joe Ward
Gunnocks, 1989

1

WHEAT, MICE AND THE CRIMEAN WAR

My grandfather, Christopher Ward, was very interested in tillage and bought 150 statute acres in Nuttstown, County Meath, in the first half of the nineteenth century. When Norman's Grove became available in 1845, he rented both the house and the land.

The land at Nuttstown was closer to Dublin than the family holdings in Fieldstown. This was important because Dublin was the market for wheat and was also the place where Christopher could get fertiliser; he could buy cow manure from the dairies on the north side of the Liffey. The manure was important because when he bought Nuttstown, it was the poorest land that a crow ever flew over, by the standards of this part of the country. Christopher did a tremendous amount of hard work, put a tremendous amount of manure on it and got it into very good shape. He also tilled the land at Norman's Grove, which was another seventy-five acres. He married my grandmother, Miss Catherine Cuffe, in 1849. The Cuffes were a landed County Dublin family.

Christopher had nine cousins living in Gunnocks. None of the seven sisters or two brothers married. This seems to be a trait of the Ward family. They probably did not want to divide the land and the women would have needed dowries to get married. Often just one of the men got married to keep the family name going. Eventually my father inherited Gunnocks and he moved from Norman's Grove to Gunnocks.

Cultivating the land for corn crops was very difficult at the time, because there was no artificial manure. The Wards used as much farm manure as they could, but it only went a limited distance because they also needed the manure to grow potatoes. The potatoes were not only for themselves, but also for the men who worked on the place. They were also able to get manure from the dairy yards in Dublin. But even with all of that, they had to leave some of the land fallow for one year in rotation, in order to get reasonably good crops. This meant that they tilled it, cultivated it and sowed no crop in it.

The cultivating was done by the men who worked at Gunnocks and who had houses on the farm. Their houses were built from a yellow clay that you find in various places around here and it was mixed with bullocks' blood, which they bought from butchers. When the blood and clay were mixed it was the same as cement. The houses were thatched and warm and comfortable, in a simple way.

England depended on Irish wheat during the first half of the nineteenth century, but this changed rapidly in the years immediately before and after the Great Famine, which took place between 1845 and 1848.

The industrial revolution at the end of the eighteenth century meant that the cities of England had come to depend on the Irish countryside for food. The Napoleonic Wars made it difficult for the British to import wheat from any country but Ireland. The British also had a protectionist food policy – known as the Corn Laws – which ensured high prices for wheat.

Wheat production is labour-intensive and provided employment for huge numbers of labourers. Between 1800 and 1845, the Irish population increased from five million to eight and a half million people. Many of these people were cottiers and landless labourers, who had little or no land of their own, but who worked for farmers and landlords. These people subsisted from the potatoes they could grow on tiny holdings, as well as the cash they could earn as seasonal agricultural workers.

The potato crop failed between 1845 and 1848. Between five hundred thousand and one million people died from hunger and disease during the Famine. Another one million people emigrated to Great Britain, the United States, Canada and Australia. The situation received international attention, with aid coming from places as exotic and dispersed as Calcutta, and from the Choctaw Indian nation in the United States.

The response of the British government was slow, inefficient and handicapped by ideological blindnesses. The British Prime Minister, Sir Robert Peel, repealed the Corn Laws to facilitate the import of cheaper foreign grain into Ireland and began to supply maize to the country. The repeal of the Corn Laws was enacted over a three-year period from 1846 to 1849 and did little to relieve the starving population.

Peel was succeeded by Lord John Russell, who focused on the provision of support through 'public works' projects. Many of these projects were pointless or wasteful, such as the construction of roads that went nowhere, the flattening of hills and the filling of valleys.

Eventually, a soup-kitchen network was established to replace the public-works projects. In the final years of the Famine, these kitchens fed more than three million people.

Potatoes were not the only source of food in Ireland, but they were the only food available to cottiers and labourers who lived away from the main towns and cities. Additionally, a huge amount of Irish food was exported to England throughout the Famine. Much of this food was exported from prosperous regions where the Famine had relatively little local effect. However, food was also shipped from some of the most famine-stricken parts of Ireland, particularly in the south and west of the country.

The most notable difference between the Great Famine and other famines around the world is that it occurred within the United Kingdom, which was the most prosperous and industrialised country in the world. British government policy was inefficient, misguided and half-hearted. Other factors, such as poor communications, the lack of transport infrastructure and the inefficiencies of local government, exacerbated the situation.

The Great Famine and its consequences are widely blamed on the indifference of the British government to its Irish subjects. There was also a significant segment of the British body politic who saw a reduction in Ireland's population as a favourable outcome and who were happy to let nature take its course. The Famine strengthened the belief among Irish nationalists – both in Ireland and the US – that Britain was not fit to rule Ireland.

For more than 150 years after the Famine, it was widely believed that the British had seized on the 'opportunity' of the Great Famine to wipe out Irish people, and the Famine is sometimes referred to as the 'Irish holocaust'. It was also widely taught in Catholic schools that Protestant proselytisers had exploited starving people by forcing them to convert to Protestantism in exchange for food. Although incidents of such abuse took place, they were not a policy of the Protestant churches.

The Famine triggered the first wave of mass emigration from Ireland. Another million people emigrated from Ireland in the second half of the nineteenth century, and by the early 1900s, a combination of emigration and a low rate of marriage had reduced the population of Ireland to four and a half million. The people who remained behind married later in life - country folk usually waited until after they had inherited the family farm. The younger members of a farm family could either emigrate or remain unmarried at home.

The Great Famine also had profound consequences for Irish agriculture. After the

17

repeal of the Corn Laws, it no longer made commercial sense to grow wheat, so farmers began to raise cattle instead, reducing the need for agricultural labourers. The number of cottiers fell from 300,000 to 88,000 over the course of the Famine. The number of farmers who had more than thirty acres increased from 50,000 to 150,000 over the same period. This pattern continued over the second half of the nineteenth century, and it was not lost on the increasingly politicised Irish population that, as the number of cattle in the country increased, the number of people living on the island decreased.

The price of wheat rocketed in the early years of the nineteenth century, during the Napoleonic War. Napoleon prevented all corn, of any kind, from getting into England by holding the European coast.

It happened again during the Crimean War in the 1850s. All of the wheat for Britain and Europe came from southern Russia and the Ukraine through the port of Odessa, from where it was shipped through the Mediterranean and out into the Atlantic. When the Bosporus – the entrance to the Black Sea – was sealed off, it was impossible for any wheat to get out into the Mediterranean. There was an absolute famine for bread-making wheat both in England and in Ireland.

During both the Napoleonic and Crimean Wars, the Ward family would have made a great deal of money from wheat. They also grew oats for the horses, although I don't think that they grew much barley.

My father told me that all of Bracetown, which is the land on both sides of the Dublin—Navan road in front of Gunnocks, was in wheat and when it was sold in Dublin, in the spring of one particular year, the price kept going up and up and up. The last one or two loads that were sent out from Gunnocks made five pounds per barrel. A barrel would have been twenty stone in weight and it was amazing to think that it would have made as much as five pounds per barrel. I have no idea what that would be worth now, because the value of a pound has fallen so much since then.

There were not many people around here to harvest a very large area of land, because everybody else had corn as well. So the county Cavan and Leitrim men – who had very small holdings – walked down to this part of the country and did the harvesting with reaping hooks. Now this was arranged in the following way: most of these men could not read or write, but there would be one man in the locality where they came from

– say Arva or Dowra or somewhere like that – who would be able to write. During my grandfather's and my father's time, they would write to this man to make the arrangements.

My father used to write to a man named O'Reilly up on the borders of Leitrim and Cavan and arrange with him that his corn would be fit on such and such a date – we'll say the fifteenth of September. O'Reilly would also have got letters from other people and some of these people would say that their corn would be fit for reaping on the first of September and somebody else maybe on the tenth. O'Reilly would come down with the men and make all the arrangements about wages. You paid the foremen and he paid the others. I never heard my father saying that there was any dispute over it.

Part of the arrangement was that you put the men up, so you kept sufficient clean straw from the previous year in the big barn for the men to sleep on.

I think that between twenty to thirty men came to the Gunnocks each year. They were very well fed, with plenty of bacon, potatoes and cabbage provided by the Wards and served on huge pewter dishes and plates. They always brought one man as a cook and he served the bacon, potatoes and cabbage with buttermilk, which was provided in large pewter jugs. If the weather was fine, trestle tables were put outside the old cow house, down near the pond.

They also brought one or two musicians with them and in the evening you could hear them playing the fiddle and entertaining one another by singing. They were as happy as can be.

On one occasion, on a certain date in September, word came down from their own part of the country to say that their own corn was fit to cut and for them to come home at once. These men were not educated, and the moment they got word, they were anxious to stop working immediately and start walking home. It took a good deal of persuasion to get them to finish the last acres. It wasn't a matter of them looking for more money or anything like that; it was just the urge to get home at once to do their own corn. However, if you had twenty or thirty acres to cut and they went away, then you wouldn't be able to cut it and that was that.

On the evening when word came that their corn was fit, there were still seventy-three acres to be cut in the mountain division field and the gate field. It was all ready and ripe to cut but they told my father that they were leaving in the morning. He said to them, 'Ah, don't go until you've finished this', but they said that they must go. He reasoned with them and, with O'Reilly's help, they said that they would start work at the first light of day.

'Have the breakfast ready for us on top of the double ditch between the mountain and Boravy,' they said.

As Laurence had agreed, he was there with bowls of porridge and milk first thing in the morning. He handed one to each man as he crossed the bank into the next field. I don't know if they had bread, but I presume that they had. They started into Boravy and had just finished it by nightfall, which indeed was a tremendous feat.

My father told me that he walked with those men up the main Dublin to Navan road, where Drummonds grain yard is now. He described to me how the sun was just going down on the western horizon and the men were all delighted with themselves as they started to walk through the night to their homes in Leitrim and Cavan.

They all called goodbye to him and said 'See you again next year'. As they went down the road they started to sing and he stood there for quite a long while listening to the ring of their hobnailed boots on the hard surface of the road and their singing in unison as they went away in the direction of Paceland and away back home to County Leitrim.

The Penal Laws – which were introduced by the British in 1690 to deny the Catholic majority in Ireland access to land, education, the professions and political influence – were repealed between the 1780s and 1829. Some of the laws were repealed by the exclusively Protestant Irish Parliament in Dublin, before it was abolished under the Act of Union in 1800. The most important remaining Penal Law – the law which forbade Catholics from sitting in the House of Commons – was repealed in 1829 as a result of a peaceful mass movement led by Daniel O'Connell.

Daniel O'Connell, known as 'The Liberator', was Ireland's leading political figure in the first half of the nineteenth century. He championed the cause of Irish Catholics – who made up almost eighty percent of the population – by campaigning for Catholic emancipation and repeal of the parliamentary union between Ireland and Great Britain.

He was born in County Kerry to a wealthy Catholic family. He studied in France and trained as a lawyer. When the United Irishmen rose against the British in 1798,

O'Connell chose not to support them because he opposed political violence. In the 1810s, he set up the Catholic Association to campaign for Catholic emancipation. The association was funded by membership dues of one penny per month, in order to attract a mass following among the poorest Irish Catholics. The money was used to fund pro-emancipation candidates for parliament.

In 1828, O'Connell ran for the parliament seat in County Clare vacated by William Vesey Fitzgerald, a Protestant who supported the Catholic Association. O'Connell won the seat but was unable to take it because of his refusal to take an oath to the King as head of the Church of England. This created a huge political problem for the Prime Minister, the Duke of Wellington, who was from Trim, in County Meath. Both the Prime Minister and his Home Secretary, Sir Robert Peel, were opposed to Catholic emancipation. However, they believed that denying O'Connell his seat would lead to civil unrest and could even provoke a rebellion in Ireland. Therefore Peel and Wellington managed to convince George IV to open Parliament to people of all Christian faiths, including Catholics. Jews and other non-Christians were granted the right to sit in Parliament in 1858.

One of the most unpopular features of the Penal Laws remained in force, however: Catholics still had to pay tithes to the Anglican Church. A campaign of non-violent resistance to the tithes – which sometimes flared into violence – was waged between 1831 and 1836.

O'Connell also campaigned for repeal of the 1800 Act of Union, which merged the parliaments of Britain and Ireland to form the United Kingdom. He set up the Repeal Association, which campaigned for the restoration of an independent Kingdom of Ireland to govern itself, with Queen Victoria as the Queen of Ireland. He organised huge rallies, which were attended by hundreds of thousands of people. The biggest of these rallies was to be held at the Hill of Tara, in County Meath. The British government banned the rally and jailed O'Connell. After the failure of his mass movement, O'Connell made little progress towards Irish independence.

He died in 1847, at the end of the Great Famine. He is remembered in Ireland as the founder of non-violent Irish nationalism and for his ability to mobilise the Catholic population as an effective political force.

I'm sure everyone knows what 'tithes' and the 'Tithe Wars' were. The tithes were a religious tax, which meant that every tenth sheaf of wheat had to be given to the clergy of the Church of Ireland in the district, regardless of the religion of the farmer producing the wheat. The Wards

3322964

were always extremely irked and very bitter at having to comply with a most unfair practice. They had quite an amount to do with the doing away of the tithes in this part of the country, in east County Meath and north County Dublin.

My grandfather – Christopher Ward – owned Nuttstown and Strokestown (which are still in the extended Ward family) when the Tithe War was at its height. All of this land was in corn at the time. Christopher had to notify the parson's man that he was reaping the corn, so that the parson's man could come along as the sheaves of corn were being threshed, or as they were being put into a rick. Every tenth one was thrown to one side and the parson's man gathered it and built it into a stack, or threw it into a cart.

My grandfather notified all the local people around – the labouring men, their wives and their children – and told them that they were to come along at the given hour that the parson's man would be there. When each of the sheaves was thrown out, two or three of them would rush in, grab it and run away with it to prevent the parson's man from getting the sheaves. This meant that Christopher could not be blamed in any way for not delivering the sheaves of corn, because he and his men threw them out to the parson's man and they were stolen by local people. The exercise was most successful and it put a stop to the practice of giving every tenth sheaf to the parson.

My great-granduncle, Christopher Ward of Fieldstown West, who was born in 1771 and died in 1845, played a large part in the Tithe Wars. We don't know very much about his involvement, but we know that he refused to pay his tithes: a sum of around £170. I think that the name of the man who took him to court was the Reverend Marcus Short. Christopher was imprisoned in the debtors' prison in Thomas Street in Dublin when aged about sixty-two. He remained there for some time, and when he was released he was presented with a silver cup, on which was engraved: 'Presented by the General Association of Ireland to Christopher Ward Esquire as a testimonial of their sympathy for his suffering in the cause of his country and as a mark of their respect for his patriotism, 1837'.

God Save the Queen
Loyal National Repeal Association of Ireland
Catholic Dissenter Protestant Quis Separabit 1782
It was and shall be
Mr William Ward, having enrolled 20 repealers, admitted as a Member of the
Association the 17th Day of June 1844
Tho. Mat.w Ray, Secretary, No. 45982
Domestic Legislation will be obtained by Peace and Perseverance
Legislative Independence of Ireland 1782
Disabilities of Dissenters Removed 1825
Catholic Emancipation 1829
Repeal _____

There are in Europe only six States having a larger population and revenue than Ireland. They are France, Russia, Austria, England, Prussia and Spain. There are sixteen independent states in Europe having less population and revenue than Ireland. They are Naples, Sardinia, Bavaria, Belgium, Portugal, Sweden, Holland, the Popedom, Switzerland, Denmark, Hanover, Saxony, Wurtemberg, Tuscany, Baden, Greece, not reckoning several minor states in Germany, Hungary. Nor even any of the United States which each have local parliaments.

But Ireland has not a parliament.

The population of Ireland was in 1841 8,175,124. Its surface covers 20,808,377 Statute acres. The annual revenue (exclusive of uncredited taxation) averages about L4,500,000. Its local taxation exceeds L2,000,000 per annum. It possesses great natural resources, in its fine harbours and in its advantageous position, capabilities for a fine commerce. Its people are intelligent, temperate, laborious and brave. Yet its agriculture languishes, its trade is paralysed, its mineral resources are unproductive, its fisheries are neglected, it is stripped of a large part of its revenue of rents and its capital. Its population is divided and impoverished.

Because Ireland has not a parliament.

At that time, corn was reaped by hand and tied up in small sheaves, or stooked. The sheaves of corn were built up on granite stands, which were brought from Wicklow, where men were experts in cutting granite.

Six or eight granite pillars were set in a circle, buried eighteen inches into the ground with another thirty inches above ground. A granite cap was placed on each pillar, which looked exactly like a mushroom cap. Timber beams or railway sleepers were placed on top of the mushroom caps, criss-crossed between the pillars. The sheaves were built on top of those into stacks. The stacks were thin on the bottom and then they jutted out in the middle and tapered away into a spire at the top. Some weeks after it had settled down, it was thatched with straw from the year before, which made it absolutely weatherproof.

The idea of the mushroom-shaped cap was to prevent mice from getting into the stacks. It made them absolutely mouse-proof, because although the mouse could run up the pillar, he couldn't walk upside down along the bottom of the granite cap. He would hit his head on the cap and fall back down onto the ground.

The only time a mouse got into the stack was when the men occasionally left a ladder or a pitchfork against one of the stacks overnight. That wouldn't happen very often I can assure you, and I've seen scores of times when there was never a mouse in them.

Supposing a mouse did get into them, or if two mice got into them, they were certain to breed and you would have ended up with quite a number of them in the stack. A mouse would have had any amount to eat, but it was all very dry food and he would get thirsty from eating dry wheat all of the time. So he bored a hole to the outside of the stack, where he cut a little eave. It was beautifully done and when it rained he was able to put his tongue out under each of the straws for the water to run down into his mouth. He didn't need a lot of water, so he had a grand fresh clean drink any time it rained.

You'd be able to see the mouse door and the eave going across, cut by his teeth. If there were more of them it could mean that a considerable amount of damage was done to the sheaves. These sheaves were not threshed until November and the last of them wouldn't be trashed until April, particularly if they were oat sheaves.

Oats weren't thrashed until April, because the germination rate was far higher if it was left in the stack than if you threshed it in October, November or December and stored it in a grain loft. That is not very practical nowadays, but it was an excellent idea and you had a one hundred percent germination rate when you took it out of the stack.

Loyal National Repeal Association of Ireland
God Save the Queen
Mr Christopher Ward, Gunnocks
Enrolled 20 Repealers, admitted as a Member of the Association
The 7th Day of May, 1841
T.M. Ray, Secretary
No. 4191

Wheat prices fell very quickly after the Napoleonic and Crimean Wars, as England and the rest of Europe were able to get wheat from the Ukraine through the port of Odessa on the Black Sea. Some of the people who were growing wheat in a big way in Ireland got their fingers badly burnt.

This didn't happen to the Wards, who threshed it and sold it every week of every month and didn't keep any carry-over – surplus or stock-piled wheat. But some people were caught with a lot of corn on their hands and had to sell at a very bad price, or found it impossible to give it away.

I do know that the Thompson family, who lived in Hollywood Rath House, got very badly caught. They were very large landowners and land-lords, owning most of the land between Kilbride and Hollywood Rath crossroads, on both sides of the road. They owned all of the land from Powerstown to Strokestown, which would include Mayne, where our neighbour Mrs Brennan lives. They owned the land surrounding Gunnocks that now belongs to the Wilkinsons, Raymond Keogh, Denis Coakley and George Wells. They also owned the other side of the road, which has since been divided into smallholdings by the Land Commission. I should imagine that they had a great deal more land as well and it was all in tillage, because that was the crop that paid in this part of the country.

The Thompsons asked Captain Armit, who owned Norman's Grove before the Wards rented it, if he would allow them to stack some of their corn in the three acres of his land that runs along by the bleach green. (A bleach green was a field used for bleaching flax for linen production – the flax was laid out across the field, exposed to the weather which helped it to turn white.)

The Thompsons put stacks upon stacks upon stacks of wheat into Captain Armit's field. It was the produce of hundreds of acres of land, from George Wells' land, the land from Rowan crossroads and Raymond Keogh's land.

If you weren't leaving the sheaves in the field for long, then the practice was to build the stacks on the ground, putting bushes or furze under them to keep the bottom sheaves from getting damp. Because corn prices had fallen, they ended up leaving the sheaves in the field for a number of years. They thatched them and did everything they could to preserve them, but prices kept falling and falling and they couldn't bring themselves to sell it. After a considerable number of years they decided to cut their losses and thresh it.

Two men went up onto the stacks, using ladders, to take off the thatch, which was held on with wrangles (wooden pins) in the same way as a house is thatched. The men were to remove the thatch, which would be taken away for use as animal bedding. The stacks looked perfect, but one of the men disappeared as he began to pull the wrangles off. The other men realised that he had fallen down through the stack, and started to pull as quickly as they could to get him out before he smothered.

Each of the stacks was absolutely infested with rats, which had chopped and chopped and eaten everything, leaving only a big heap of dust. But they hadn't damaged the outer frame of the stack, which was now only a shell. The men tried the other stacks and found that each of them was the same.

In the second half of the nineteenth century, the era of corn production came to an end and the Wards of Gunnocks, Nuttstown and Fieldstown turned to the keeping of cattle and sheep. One of the reasons why people abandoned tillage was the fact that England began importing cheap American wheat, oats and Indian corn or maize.

The country people in Ireland called the maize 'yella male', because it was terribly hard and formed a yellow meal once it was ground down to be fed to people or animals. It certainly had a great deal of nutrition and filling properties.

During the famine in the 1840s, there were official government soup kitchens and in a few places, particularly in Mayo, kitchens set up by evangelical Protestant groups. The proselytisers – 'the soupers' – used to boil this yellow meal and dish it out to the poverty-stricken people. It certainly kept them alive for some time, although it was a despicable type of thing to do, because people had to renounce their Catholic religion and become nominal Protestants in order to receive the food. In most cases they renounced their Protestant religion as soon as they had their dinner eaten.

I often think to myself – I shouldn't be talking about these things, I suppose – I think it's no wonder that the Protestant religion never took well in Ireland if they tried to convert the people by that means.

The land that had been in corn was laid down in grass. Some of it was never laid down; it just came back into grass. Tradition says that the big meadow on Rooske farm, which belongs to the people of the parish, was never laid down. It is one of the best fields in the area. That grass had to be used, so people bought cattle and sheep and put them onto it.

My father and my Uncle Michael went into partnership, renting land and buying cattle together. The Thompsons let all of their lands go back into grass and father initially rented Rowan and some of both Mayne and Boravy from them.

The Thompsons, who lived on the far side of Dublin in Rathfarnham, were gentlemanly people. They eventually set all of that land to my father and uncle at a very reasonable rent because they knew that they would never give them any trouble.

2

CHRISTOPHER AND JOHN'S FAIR DAYS

My grandfather, who was born in the first decade of the nineteenth century, was a very devout man. In those days people only received the Blessed Sacrament once a year, or at most twice a year.

In Christopher's case, he received twice: once at Christmas and once at Easter. He regarded the receiving of Holy Communion so strictly that for a week beforehand he locked himself into his bedroom to pray. He only came down to meals and he hardly spoke at the table. For the week after he received, he locked himself into his room for a whole week in thanksgiving for receiving Holy Communion.

This was a very strict interpretation of Catholic teaching, even at that time. In fact, I think it was outré, if I might use that expression. His son, Father John Ward, was a theologian – and a good one at that – and I remember him saying that his father was 'tarred with Jansenism' – which was a strict interpretation of Catholicism that was not in keeping with orthodox Catholicism.

Christopher Ward had a very strict standard with regard to the keeping of Sunday and I imagine he was stricter than other Catholics were. I think that he interpreted the keeping of Sunday very much as the strict Protestant or Calvinist idea.

He also impressed his ideas upon his sons and they kept Sunday strictly as well. I don't mean that they didn't play moderate games, or that they wouldn't play cards. I would even imagine that they possibly had a certain amount of dancing on Sundays.

However, he would neither buy nor sell nor transact any kind of business on a Sunday. As well as that, he did not allow himself, his sons, or the workmen to work on the farm on a Sunday, other than for necessary things such as milking or harnessing the horse and that kind of thing.

As a last extreme, he would allow the men to work at the hay or the harvest if it was the end of the hay season, or if it was a wet year for the harvest. In all cases, they would have to go to mass first, get their breakfast and then come along for the work.

On one occasion, Christopher was very busy with the hay or with the harvest and when it came to Sunday he decided to go over to Mister Wilkinson in Powerstown and pay him the rates.

The Wilkinsons were – and still are – an extremely strict family and are very strict with regard to the Sunday observance. When he told Wilkinson that he was there to pay the rates, Wilkinson said that he would not accept money on a Sunday and that he should come back some other day during the week. I think that my grandfather was always terribly ashamed of making such a faux pas as that, particularly with a Protestant family.

The Wilkinsons have since moved from Powerstown to Tyrrellstown, but before they lived in Powerstown they lived near Tara, where they had a very big farm, house and farm buildings.

After the Battle of Tara in 1798, a great many of the people retreating after the battle took refuge in the Wilkinsons' hay barns and outhouses. Of course, the Wilkinsons knew they were there and when the Yeomen and British army came to search the place, the Wilkinsons told them that they were loyal to the Crown and that there was no need to search their premises. The Yeomen left without searching and quite a number of rebels, or insurgents, or whatever you like to call them, were saved.

The 1798 rebellion was organised by the United Irishmen, a republican group inspired by the egalitarian principles of the American and French Revolutions. The movement was strongest among Presbyterians and Catholics, who wanted to establish an independent Irish republic and to abolish the privileges enjoyed only by the members of the Church of Ireland.

Molly Weston and her brothers were organisers for the United Irishmen in north County Dublin and south County Meath. Following the outbreak of the rebellion in Kildare, the Meath and north Dublin rebels assembled at the Hill of Tara, because of its historical and cultural symbolism, as well as its commanding view of the surrounding countryside. On her journey to the Hill of Tara, Molly mustered men and women from the villages along the way, including Oldtown, Garristown, Curragha, Ratoath and Dunshaughlin.

The Tara rebels successfully attacked a party of Reay Fencibles militia, who were on their way to Dublin. The Fencibles summoned reinforcements and counterattacked in an engagement known as the Battle of Tara. Molly is reported to have ridden a white horse throughout the battle while she rallied the rebels and led them in charges against the British troops. Eventually the British gained the upper hand, and five hundred rebels were killed before the battle was over. The four Weston brothers were killed in the battle; Molly's body was never found.

My grandfather, Christopher Ward, and his brother John used to travel to fairs all around the country to buy cattle. In those days there were fewer cattle fairs, and people travelled to the fairs on foot, by horse and cart, or on the barge canals.

In the 1820s, they bought and sold cattle in Ardeath, Bective, Balbriggan, Celbridge, Drogheda, Kilsallaghan, Swords and Fieldstown. The latter fair was held each year on Ward's farm on the last day of May. The field on which the fair was held is still called the 'fair green field'.

Some of the cattle sold at these fairs were brought long distances by dealers. In 1820, they bought thirteen cows from William Walsh of Maryborough, County Laois. Other cattle were bought in Celbridge from Dan Lawlor, who was from Mountrath in Laois.

In the early decades of the nineteenth century, some of the Wards used to drive a horse and trap and a man – either Mick Phoenix or Mick Geoghegan – down to Knockcroghery in County Roscommon. It was a long journey in a horse and cart and they had to pay tolls and the cost of putting up themselves and their man for the night.

They also used to attend fairs in Ballymahon in Longford and Multyfarnham in County Meath. They took the canal boat from Kilcock to Lanesborough and finished their journey by car.

My grandfather and John used to travel from Kilcock down to Ballinasloe on the 'fly boats', as they were called. These canal barges went to the Great Fair of Ballinasloe, where as many as ten thousand cattle were sold on the Friday of the first week in October. The sheep fair, which was held on Wednesday, was immense: there were as many as a hundred thousand sheep on the fair green. The sheep were bought in big lots, with no less than one hundred sheep in each lot. Sometimes there could be as many as five hundred sheep in a lot, but I know that the Wards didn't buy that many.

The sheep at the fair were the Galway-Roscommon breed, which were pretty much the same as the Galways are today. In those days, sheep weren't sold until they were three or four years old because people wanted much bigger sheep than they want now. They wanted more meat on the sheep and more fat.

The sheep that were bought for Gunnocks were wethers, which was the term for a castrated male sheep. The females and their lambs were kept in the west of Ireland and only the wethers came up to Meath.

It was unusual to keep the ewes and the lambs in those days. The cattle and sheep were bred in the west and fed in the east, so land in places like Meath was only used to fatten up animals for a few months before they were sold again. The Wards did not rear lambs. My father was the first member of the family to keep ewes and lambs, at the end of the nineteenth century. He kept them to graze the lawns of Norman's Grove, to keep down the weeds, and he only kept a few.

I would imagine that the Wards brought a tar-pot to Ballinasloe with the big 'W' brand, to mark the sheep before they put them into paddocks. The sheep were held over in sheep parks around the area, until the cattle fair took place on Friday.

Once the fair was over, the sheep were walked from Ballinasloe to Gunnocks, which is a pretty fair walk for a sheep, approximately ninety miles. My Uncle Michael told me that modern sheep would not be able to walk from Ballinasloe to Dublin. He said that they were too finely bred and hadn't the age of the sheep that they would have had in the 1840s through to the end of the nineteenth century. He told me that in the 1930s he used to walk his sheep from Kilcloon to the cattle market in Dublin, which is a distance of eighteen miles. When they got in they were very tired and they lay down for around two hours before he started putting them up for sale.

The Wards bought the wethers in October and they were fed at Gunnocks on grass until January. From January they were put on oats and barley and possibly some Indian meal. They sold them in March and April when sheep were at their scarcest and made a nice bit of profit in the Dublin market.

To the best of my belief, all of those sheep – or a good proportion of them – were eaten in the city of Dublin, although some of them were shipped to various parts of England.

Natti Reid of Ballymacoll – which adjoins Nuttstown and which is now owned by Dillons – kept ewes and lambs. One particular Easter in the 1890s, he was boasting outside the chapel in Dunboyne that he had sold a lamb for £3, which was a tremendous price. The Reids of Ballymacoll were related to the Wards.

Both the Wards in Norman's Grove and their cousins, the Wards in Fieldstown, had large families. Both families were self-sufficient in meat, flour, meal and vegetables.

Every May, they bought fifty cheviot wethers in Roundwood, County Wicklow. As a young man, my father started off early in the morning with one of the men and drove the horse and trap up to Roundwood. He didn't stay overnight, even though it's a good distance from here.

They would buy the sheep in one lot, so that they would stay together when you were bringing them home. As everybody knows, a Wicklow cheviot is not too easy to drive until he gets tired. That's why a few drovers were employed along with the man from Gunnocks for the first two or three miles, until the sheep got tired. Then they paid off the drovers and walked the sheep home from Roundwood to Gunnocks. They were rested for a week or two in Gunnocks and then half of them were walked over to Fieldstown.

One of those sheep would be killed and dressed every alternate week; one in Fieldstown, the other killed in Norman's Grove. The meat was then divided between the two houses. At Christmas-time they killed a good lean Kerry bullock, which they'd bought in Dublin. Some of that meat would be distributed among all of the workmen and other people that would be around the place, like the families of workmen, etc.

My father always said that the sheep that was killed in Fieldstown had a much better flavour than the Norman's Grove sheep that was fattened in Nuttstown. However, I know from my own experience that Nuttstown is marvellous land for fattening sheep, particularly Tobberara. There's a big division – a field or a set of inter-connected fields – there and you could fatten anything on it.

The cattle fair at Ballinsloe took place from Thursday until Saturday. The cattle that came from Kerry and the south were sold on the Thursday of the fair. The Galway, Mayo, Sligo and Clare cattle were sold on the Friday. Anything that was left over was sold to the local farmers on Saturday, on what was called the 'farmer's day'.

The horse fair was held early in the week, on Tuesday. The Ward's men, who came down on the canal boat to drive the cattle home, would always ask John and Christopher to buy a horse.

It wasn't that they wanted to ride it home, they just wanted to throw their coats over it as they walked along the road. The Ward's men and Captain Armit's men walked together, with a big drove of sheep and heifers and a horse carrying half a dozen men's coats. The horse might be useful as a hunter, or if he was young he might make a good farm horse.

My relation by marriage, Captain Maurice O'Connell, who was a grandson of Daniel O'Connell, told me that the cattle from Derrynane in Kerry were walked 180 miles to Ballinasloe up to the 1960s. He said that they were the freshest cattle walking into the big fair green. He didn't claim that they were the best cattle in Ballinasloe, but that they were the freshest and the fittest on their feet. He thought it was because they were fed on the strand and on the islands at Derrynane. These were big old cattle, which weighed around nine hundredweight.

The Derrynane cattle that I used to buy, in the twentieth century, travelled in luxury. They were taken forty miles in a lorry to Killarney and loaded into a train which brought them to Dublin, a total trip of around twelve hours. When we took them off at the Cabra railway station, they went like billy-o down the North Circular Road; they were very healthy animals.

One of the sellers who sold cattle to my grandfather was a man called Tully, from Ballinagate in Roscommon, not far from Castlereagh. The

Wards always bought Tully's cattle, so he used to bring them in especially for them and he knew the kind they wanted. On the morning of the fair, they went straight to him and they made their deals.

There is a hotel in Castlereagh that belonged to a family of Tullys. When I asked the owner about them, he told me that his family used to live out in the country, not as far as Ballinagate, but it's likely they were the same family.

The Wards bought cattle from other people as well, because fairs were not usual at that time and they wanted to buy as many as possible. They would have bought one hundred or maybe one hundred and fifty cattle in Ballinasloe.

The great October fair in Ballinasloe was more than just a place for the buying and selling of cattle, sheep and horses. It was also a great social event for the people who attended the fair. The men who worked at Gunnocks regarded it as a week's holiday, and fun and games were had by everybody. Each evening there were card games for high stakes, singing, dancing, all kinds of amusements and – of course – drinking in a big way.

Christopher and John brought their best clothes with them on the fly boat and attended functions every night for the whole week of the fair. The Wards were people of good standing in the county, they were educated and they would have met a great many of the gentlemen of similar standing in Ballinasloe. These people would have come from Galway, Roscommon, Clare and Mayo.

At that particular time, the Ward family fed only heifers and evidently had a good trade for them. These were short-horn heifers, reds, rowans and white ones, which they bought when they were four years old. They were big, heavy, strong heifers with horns, which were sold off at between eleven hundredweight and eleven and a half hundredweight.

In the time of Christopher and John Ward, these cattle would have had extremely long horns, because they were bred differently. The idea of breeding them down to the smaller horn had not come in at that time.

They outwintered most of these cattle on the land but picked out fifty of the best of them to put them into sheds in Nuttstown in December.

They were tied by chains in the sheds and were fed oats, barley and South American cake. This cake came from Paraguay and Uruguay; it was very cheap and very fattening. After the cattle had been fed on it for a few weeks, you could rub their coats and the oil would come off in your hands. They also made sure to have the last of them sold on the week of 17 March, the week in which Saint Patrick's Day fell.

They didn't start to sell the out-wintered animals until the last week in June, when they were walked in to the old Dublin cattle market in Smithfield, where they were ringed up loose. In order to get the cattle to stand in a ring, they gave them a certain amount of beating, until they all got their heads together. Then a group of around twenty would stand there with their tails out and would stand patiently for four or five hours without stirring. In fact, it was quite hard to break them up once they had been sold and were to be driven away.

Although the Wards bought most of their heifers in Ballinasloe, they also used to travel on the canal boats to the fair in Birr. They used to leave early in the morning on the canal boat, to arrive in at Dooley's Hotel in Birr at around noon. It's a very old hotel, but it's still there.

On one occasion the hotel porter asked them whether they would be having lunch. They said that they would and he asked them if they'd like to have turkey. It was September or early October and the turkey would have been very nice, so they were delighted with the idea of having turkey for lunch.

While they were up in the room having a wash and taking off their clothes, one of them looked out through the window to see the hall porter in the yard, where there was a big flock of turkeys. He was carrying a big knife and was watching to catch one of the turkeys to kill it for the lunch. I hardly need to tell you that the turkey would have been rather tough after catching and killing it straight away.

So they threw up the window and shouted 'Spare its life, we'll have the roast mutton instead!'

Licence to carry and have Arms in a Proclaimed District
I, Thomas Desuccy, having been duly appointed in that behalf, under an Act passed in the Eleventh Year of the Reign of Her Majesty Queen Victoria, intituled, 'An Act for the better prevention of Crime and Outrage in certain parts of Ireland, until the First day of December, One Thousand Eight Hundred and Forty-nine, and to the end of the then next Session of Parliament,' do hereby grant to John Ward of Gunnocks a Licence to carry and have two guns and five pistols within the County of Meath.

Dated this 1st day of August 1848.
Thomas Desuccy RM

After a number of years, the railways were built, and a number of other fairs started up throughout the country. One of the biggest fairs was in Moate, in County Westmeath. I have the old account books of John Ward going there to buy cattle from people from north Tipperary, around Roscrea and Nenagh. On another occasion they bought cattle in Boyle in Roscommon as well.

I have nothing more to say about my grandfather and John Ward with regard to the attendance at fairs and markets. But I will tell you something about Captain Armit, whose men used to walk back from Ballinasloe with the Wards.

Captain Armit lived in Norman's Grove in the 1830s and 1840s. He was a sporting character, a hard rider to hounds, a hard drinker and a wife beater. I would think that he was a man of his time.

He kept deer in the back yard for his sporting activities. In those days the walls around the yards in Norman's Grove were higher than they are now. He used to drive the deer along a passage by the yard into a deer cart, shutting the gate behind them. His hounds were kept in the house where Lillie Hynes used to live at Norman's Grove, which was the huntsman's house at the time.

The big pond at the end of the back lawn had been dug out by hand, filled with water and used to keep the food for the hounds, such as dead horses, cattle and sheep. The water was high enough so other animals couldn't get in to eat it.

Armit kept a number of men 'on the table', which means that they were fed and perhaps housed as well. My grandfather saw them at tea once and said that each man had a slab of butter and a loaf of bread in front of him. However, one man kept his loaf under his arm the whole time, only taking it out to cut a slice off it. Grandfather did not ask why, nor was he told.

Armit's men were all big and strong, a qualification that they had to keep while they worked in Norman's Grove. When a new man was employed, he had to have a boxing match with the Captain. After tea the tables and chairs in the big stone-flagged kitchen were pushed back. Armit and the new man stripped, except for their trousers, and boxed with bare fists till one or other was beaten. If the Captain won, the man was fired at once, but if the man won then he secured the job. It's likely that Armit lost the boxing match fairly often, because he had a large number of men and he would have had none if he'd won every match.

Every now and then Armit went on the beer. When he was in that state, he used to beat his wife with a horse whip. She knew from experience when this attack was about to happen, so she used to get out through the door at the back of the house through which the coal was brought into the kitchen. She used to run across the fields to the Widow Ward's shop nearby at Ballymagillan, where the stud farm is now. She used to stay with the widow, who was not related to us, until she had word that the Captain was all right again and then she returned home.

Armit was a member of the English garrison in Dublin and he left Ireland in 1845 to live in England, having set the house to my grandfather. It will not surprise my readers to learn that he was 'put' into a lunatic asylum in Nottingham in the 1860s and died there over one hundred years ago. The Wards bought the house and land at the end of the nineteenth century.

3

LAURENCE AND HIS BROTHERS

My father, his three brothers – John, Patrick and Michael – and their sister, Mary Jane, were educated at home by a tutor, a Mister O'Halloran. He was a native of Kerry who had previously worked as a tutor to the Marquis of Lansdowne when he lived in Kenmare.

Mister O'Halloran lived in the house and had a specially fitted out schoolroom in the yard. I remember the blackboard and the desks in an upstairs room in one of the farm buildings.

He was an outstanding tutor who taught them not only all the normal subjects of the time but also Latin and Greek. He used to take them for walks around the locality, where he taught them the names of the various birds, frogs, plants and grasses; everything of that kind. He taught them how to make walking sticks out of blackthorn and he even taught them to make walking sticks out of plaited ivy.

The conditions of the teachers' employment contracts were written down in a ledger, for example: 'Mr John Leyden commenced the tuition of my children May 24th 1864, he is to teach them anything that he can teach, as far as I will require, and attend to them at all times after school hours, by instruction etc. I am to pay him a salary of £25 sterling for one year, with board and lodging.'

Mister Leyden was another teacher that Christopher Ward hired to teach his four sons and daughter, whom, it seemed, learned Greek and Latin. On the debit side of the ledger, we see the withdrawals made from Leyden's account: 'To Cash going to Ratoath 2 shillings. To Cash going to Dublin £2. To Cash for medicine 1 shilling 8d.'

Whatever was left in his account at the end of the year was paid to him. Most of the people working here saved the money and spent only a few shillings during their time here.

My father told me that, when he was a boy, there were four unrelated Ward families living around Norman's Grove. The first was the Widow Ward, mentioned earlier. She ran a shop selling home-made bread, cakes and sweets, and my father and his three brothers often ran across the fields to buy things from her.

The second, Jim Ward, lived in the tall stone house that stood further along the road from the widow, beside Raymond Brady's new home. During the worst part of the Great Famine, he had a side of bacon from which he took a rasher or two each day. He did not keep the bacon in his house but hid it nearby in a stone shore – a drain – very close to Kit Barker's house.

During the 1860s, there was a huge storm in this part of the country and hundreds of trees were blown down. One day, while workmen were clearing and cutting up these trees, Jim was sitting on top of a sapling elm that had been pinned under a big beech. When the men cut the elm, the sapling sprang up and fired Jim out into the field. Strangely, he was not hurt.

Then there was the Ward family of Ruan, which was the oldest Ward family living in the district. They were known as the 'Gully' Wards, from the Irish 'Giolla'. The Ruan Wards and the Gunnocks Wards were always great friends and helped each other in many ways down through the centuries. They shared the same landlord, which was a help in terms of fixing rents and paying them at times that suited each family.

A horse fair took place in Dunboyne every year on 9 July. It was a very old fair, with its own charter, and it lasted until the end of the nineteenth century. It was on a par with the horse fair in Cahirmee, at which Napoleon's famous white charger Marengo was bought. Many of the two-year-olds bought in Dunboyne were used to 'horse' the great armies of Europe.

Although many of the horses came from County Meath and other districts, a large number came from east County Dublin. The farms in east County Dublin were smaller than in Meath and the farmers were in the market-gardening business, growing potatoes and vegetables. They kept one or two mares to work the farm and bred foals from them every year, or every second year. They sold the foals as two-year-olds, which were referred to as 'longtails'. This was because their tails had never been cut and came right down to the ground.

I've no idea of course why Dunboyne was selected for the fair, but it may be the fact that it was convenient to Dublin. Many of the buyers came from England, stayed one night in Dublin and then travelled out to Dunboyne on the train, or in a pony and trap.

The fair was held in the centre of the town, which hasn't changed since that time. The horses were 'tried' and galloped on the grass in Saint Peter's Park, in the days before trees were grown on it. When a horse was being 'tried', a man would run fifty yards with them on a lead, to show their form.

Horses were also sold singly or in groups around the park and along the roads leading into the village. There were several thousand horses in it and it was extremely dangerous. Crossing the road from Brady's pub to the green entailed a certain amount of risk, because the horses were so thickly parked on the roadway. A horse could back into you, stand on your foot, or kick you.

It was a great meeting for the local people, as well as for the people as far west as Kilcock, County Kildare, and Summerhill, County Meath, and as far east as the Irish Sea. Amid all this activity, there were vendors selling churns, furniture and fruit, although very few cattle were on offer.

If a man bought a number of horses, then he could hire a Dublin drover to lead the horses back into Dublin. They were able to bring as many as six horses at once, three on each arm. Others tied them behind carts or traps and made several trips in and out of Dublin. In some cases, they brought them straight to the boat, and in other cases they were rested for a few days before they were exported to England.

The Wards from County Dublin and the local Wards would meet at the fair, because everybody had an interest in horses, which were the only means of transport. After the fair, the members of the various Ward families had their dinner in Gunnocks.

Back around 1865, my father was sitting with his brothers on the wall at the front entrance to Norman's Grove, watching the longtails coming from east County Dublin. My father and his brothers weren't allowed to go to the fair until they were old enough to look after themselves.

The owners sat in a back-to-back trap, or a cart, and tied between two and four of these animals to the back of the cart. The longtails were either completely untrained, or partially broken. The horse that was pulling the cart would travel fast, so that the longtails had to run to keep up with the pace.

My father and his brothers loved sitting on the wall, watching these horses come galloping around the sharp bend at the back of Norman's Grove. They swept around the corner at terrific speed on their way to the fair.

After a number of years their parents decided that the brothers should go to Castleknock College, which was run by the Vincentian Fathers. My father was eighteen years old when he was sent to Castleknock, although his brothers were somewhat younger. In those days it was not unusual for a boy to go to school when he was eighteen or nineteen years old.

The priests decided that my father would be suitable to be a master of the senior boys' dormitory. However, on one occasion my father took them out for a walk, during which all of the boys got drunk. I don't think that my father was drunk, but when they returned to the school the priests noticed the other boys immediately. My father lost his position but I don't think it worried him very much.

Although his brothers stayed in Castleknock for a number of years, my father returned home after a year. After my grandfather died and my granduncle John got too old for the fairs, my father – who was the eldest son – took over from them. He started travelling around the country, buying bullocks and heifers in the fairs at Balla, Ballinasloe, Tuam and Moate.

Catholic emancipation led to a resurgence of the institutions of the Catholic Church in Ireland and expanded the political and social influence of the Catholic clergy. The Catholic Church was particularly dominant in the areas of education and hospitals.

Cardinal Paul Cullen was the dominant figure in the Irish Catholic Church through the middle of the nineteenth century, as it experienced its post-emancipation resurgence. Cullen returned to Ireland in 1850, after spending eighteen years as the rector of the Irish College in Rome. His first appointment in Ireland was as Papal Legate and Archbishop of Armagh.

When he arrived in Ireland, he organised the first National Synod since the Reformation. He introduced stricter ecclesiastical discipline into the Irish church and imposed many Roman customs which had not previously been in force. In 1852 Cullen was made Archbishop of Dublin and in 1866 became the first cardinal to be created in Ireland, where he remained until his death in 1878.

Cardinal Cullen introduced a number of new religious orders to Ireland in the 1850s. He also encouraged an upsurge in Marian devotion in Ireland, after Pope Pius IX proclaimed the dogma of the Immaculate Conception of the Blessed Virgin.

Between 1850 and 1870 there was a wave of church building throughout Ireland. The new Catholic churches were built confidently in the centre of towns and villages, with money collected from Irish-Americans, as well as from prosperous farmers, businesspeople and ordinary people.

The new churches were used for the Catholic Church's internal mission efforts. Catholics were encouraged, through pulpit oratory and formal sermons, to be more religiously observant.

According to the census of 1861, four out of five people on the island of Ireland were Catholics. Only one in eight belonged to the Church of Ireland.

Despite this, the Church of Ireland was the established church, which empowered it to collect tithes from Catholics and Presbyterians, as well as from its own members. Its ecclesiastical courts were recognised in civil law, its bishops were government nominees, and its privileged position was protected by parliament.

Catholics resented this situation, and their hostility was fuelled by Protestant evangelical proselytising missions in Ireland, financed and directed from England, between 1850 and 1870.

In 1869, the British Prime Minister introduced the Irish Church Bill, to disestablish the Church of Ireland. The bill disestablished all religions, removing government support to the Catholic university in Maynooth, as well as the annual grant given to the Presbyterian Church.

Laurence's younger brother John made up his mind to become a Vincentian priest shortly after he went to Castleknock. The priests told him a lot about the order, so by the time he left Castleknock he was quite au fait with the rules of the Vincentian order.

He was sent to the Sorbonne in Paris, where he stayed for three years. I remember saying to him once, 'I suppose you knew Paris very well', and he said, 'No, I never went any further in Paris than from our house to the Sorbonne, which was not very far.'

The chief reason for that was that the young students wore full-length cassocks and black hats and the Parisians were very anti-clerical.

John said to me that he would be walking down to or back from the Sorbonne and people would call out 'so-and-so crows', which shows that they were not popular. That's why he saw almost nothing of Paris for the three years he was over there.

When John returned to Ireland, the authorities in the seminary in Maynooth asked the Vincentians to send them a sensible priest, to be a spiritual director to the young men who were training for the priesthood. There were a great number of seminarians in Maynooth at that time and, to my mind, it was a great honour to be asked to form the minds of the young men who were going to be priests.

John took his role very seriously and my father told me that the three years he spent in Maynooth practically killed him. He never left his room except to say mass and to have his meals. The rest of the time he stayed in his room, waiting for young men to come up and ask him questions. He was worried that when a young man might be out walking on the grass, or taking a walk on the avenue, or something like that, something might come into his mind and he would go up at once to my uncle, who would tell him what he wanted to know. As John said, 'Supposing I was not in the room when that man came up, he probably would not come up again. Perhaps in twenty years' time he would be asked that particular question again and he would not be able to answer it or answer it properly.' So John felt it behove him to answer that young man's query. That's why he never left his room.

After he left Maynooth, he returned to the Vincentians in Phibsborough and was appointed to give missions throughout Ireland, encouraging Catholics to be more religiously observant. In those days, a mission was a very serious and a very big undertaking. In most of the big towns, a mission was made up of six priests. They visited every single house – every Catholic house, of course – in the parish. Some houses were visited two or three times, if the priests were not successful on the first occasion.

During the period that he was on the mission, the Church of Ireland – the Anglican Church or whatever you like to call it – was also in the fields with what they called the 'Irish Church Mission to Roman Catholics'. Most of the money subscribed to them was collected by people in London; elderly people who left large sums of money to what they called the Irish Peasant Society, or the Society for the Conversion of the

Irish Peasant. That brought in large sums of money to these church missionaries.

John said that he would come up against people who had been converted to Protestantism and he had to reason with them, to try to get them back again. He mentioned one particular case to me, when they were walking along the road and they met a fine cut of a girl coming along. They stopped to talk to her and something came out about divorce and she said 'That's all baloney'. She said that of course she could get a divorce; she had heard that from the Irish Church Mission people.

Father John Ward was an absolutely wonderful preacher and confessor. On one occasion he was so successful that the people paid for a special carriage to be put behind the main train to bring him back to Dublin. It was the assistant stationmaster in Sligo, Mister Doyle, who told me about this. John never mentioned it; he was certainly a very humble man and a man who had tremendous talents. It just goes to show how much he was appreciated in Sligo town.

Father John said that Clonmel, in County Tipperary, was one of the most difficult areas in which to give a retreat. The people were not interested and they didn't turn up for mass or for the sermons. He blamed it on the large number of Wesley Protestant houses in south Tipperary, which had a large number of staff, both indoors and outdoors. These staff would have become very lackadaisical about their religion.

I heard a story from one of his colleagues about one occasion when John was missioning in Clonmel. There was a man and a woman living together in a house and they were not married. He had visited the house twice, but he got no good out of them.

The third time he visited them, he got very worked up about what would happen to them in the next life, and was shouting at them at the top of his voice, standing in the kitchen of their house. A huge cat, which was lying in front of the fire, got fed up with the noise that John was making. He got up from the hearth, scratched himself and walked across the kitchen floor. Suddenly the cat got a heart attack and dropped dead on the floor. The man and the woman threw themselves on their knees and said, 'For God's sake, don't strike us down like you did to the cat.' So, at any rate, either he or the cat was successful in getting them back to their religion.

John usually took his holidays on the Continent and on one occasion he travelled to the Continent with my father. John said to me, at various times, 'We priests can travel anywhere in the world because we all know Latin perfectly and we can carry on our conversations in Latin.'

When they were in Germany, John and Laurence went to the parish priest of the town where they were staying and John asked permission to say mass. The priest agreed, so John asked him whether he wanted him to say mass at any particular time, because he didn't want to discommode him in any way. The priest said, 'No, well, of course – not later than six o'clock in the morning.' That would be Germans for you at that particular time, they wanted everything pretty early.

After spending a number of years on the missions in Ireland, John was appointed to be parish priest at Lanark, in Scotland. He had a small congregation, because most Scots are Presbyterian. He stayed there for quite a number of years and he did make some converts. It also happened that his church burned down and the insurance money allowed him to build a much better and nicer church in Lanark.

After a number of years in Lanark, John was recalled to Ireland to do missionary work once more. I remember him giving one retreat in Blanchardstown, in County Dublin, towards the end of his days. He was very emphatic throughout his sermon and it was a bit over my head – I had only just left school and it was very academic.

Afterwards, I went into the sacristy to see him and I remember him just lying back there in a chair, completely exhausted, taking sips of a glass of sherry. He was a man who knew wine, but at that time port and sherry were what you drank. He didn't drink whiskey until the very end of his life.

Father John was very hard on himself. He would get very wound up, emphasising some particular point, and he would roll his sleeve up, right up to the shoulder, without realising it.

He strained his larynx – that's the vocal cords – from the terrific use of them. There were no microphones at that time and you had to direct your voice so that the men standing at the back of the church could clearly hear what you were saying. That was very much a strain during missions, where he spoke twice a day for two or three weeks. It was understandable that he had strained his cords rather badly.

He did go to a Protestant clergyman in England, who said that he had a cure for it. Father John said that when you came down in the morning, he gave you an apple to eat and in the middle of the day you got something else to eat and something in the evening. The cure was starvation, rest and starvation. John was doubtful about the cure; he believed that rest and silence did more to cure his larynx.

In his latter years he was attached to Phibsborough church, where he was regarded as an outstanding confessor. On the one hand, he was a man who was extremely strict on both himself and everybody else. At the same time, he had a great way with people who took too much drink. He had quite a large number of people at the time who would take too much drink, both men and women, and they went to confession to him.

When my Uncle Michael left school, he was apprenticed to a wine merchant in Stonybatter, near the cattle markets in Dublin. He didn't like that job and would have preferred to have been farming, like my father and my Uncle Patrick, who was farming in Nuttstown.

Although they didn't have much money, my father and Michael decided to go into partnership, by renting some part of Rowan from the Thompson family. The Thompsons were the landlords whose corn had been eaten by the rats and who had let their lands go back into grass.

In the first year they bought fifty cattle, paying £5 per head. My father gave the twenty-five heifers to my uncle at £4 each and he took the bullocks for himself at £6. It just so happened that they bought the cattle in a very good year and that they doubled what they paid for them. That really started Michael off in the cattle business and eventually they rented all of Rowan from the Thompsons. Rowan would include all of Coakleys', George Wells', (the current owners) and the land on the other side of the road that was divided up years later by the Irish Land Commission, running away up to Nuttstown.

The cattle trade began to change when my father and Uncle Michael took over from Christopher and John. There was much more profit in buying calves or stripper cows, rather than buying bullocks or heifers.

Stripper cows were cows that came from the dairies in the south of Ireland, which either hadn't gone into calf or were no use as milkers. These cows were sold in the spring and they were bought in their thousands by farmers from Kildare, Meath and Dublin.

It was a bad system from the dairy man's point of view, because if a cow went dry in November – as mòst of them did – they had to keep them right through the winter until March or April before they could sell them. That meant that they had a pretty long keep on them, while the money that they got for them was pretty small.

The strippers throve extremely well and the trade at the time was very much for cheap meat. There were two reasons for this; the first was that the Belfast shipyards were working very well, and strippers provided cheap meat for the workers in the shipyards. The rest of the cows went to the industrial areas of England.

Although the meat was much cheaper than bullocks or heifers, it was still very good meat. So my father and uncles started buying cows in the south of Ireland in the springtime, particularly in County Clare. The bottom-lands of the farm that now belongs to Coakleys was always known as the 'strippers' bottoms', because the Wards fed any quantity of cows on it.

The Ward brothers had a sister, Mary Jane Ward, who received her secondary educa-tion from the Dominicans in Kingstown (Dun Laoghaire). In 1880 she won a school prize for music. When she returned to Norman's Grove, she was lonely because her mother had died, her brothers were out working and she was socially restricted because of her class and education; there would have been very few women in the area with a secondary education. She became depressed and was put into the paying section of St Vincent's Home in Fairview, Dublin, which was run by the Sisters of Charity. She spent the rest of her life in the home, where she was visited by her brothers and by Joe and Lilla Ward. In the nineteenth and for much of the twentieth century, people did not talk about family members who were in psychiatric hospitals, for fear that the entire family would be stigmatised. Mary Jane Ward wrote in a letter to John Ward:

Norman's Grove,
1871

My Dear John,

Previous to receiving your letter on the 30th it was my intention to write to Michael on that day thinking you would be too busy *pounding* for the Easter examinations to think of such a trifle as my letter. Many thanks for your inquiries about me. I am happy to inform you that I am not at all lonely. It was really time to remove the Eastern boundary. I am sure few of the boys will fret after it as it looked anything but ornamental and gave the playground too confined an appearance. I had a view of the College from the train on last Wednesday but of course the distance was too great to notice any of the recent improvements. On that day my uncle John was made Chairman of the Dunshauglin Union in place of our late M.P. Mr. Corbally. There were four Gentlemen proposed for that office amongst them was Lord Fingal but Uncle John was successful. Last week there was a Dr elected for Dunboyne. His name is Dwyer. He will take possession of the Dispensary on next Tuesday. There are still great preparations being made at the Castle for the new owner who is expected to arrive in this country in June. It is said that it contains . . . bed rooms but you know that a report loses nothing in the carriage. I intend going to see it very soon and then I will be able to form an opinion of its greatness. Arthur Green came here on Sunday. We went away to hunt with Rover and killed two large rats at the back of Caulstown They were fellows that would have been a treat to the Parisians during the siege. He intended coming over today but I am going over to Fieldstown now and purpose dining with Mr & M O'Brien this evening,

Mary

4

LAURENCE'S FAIR DAYS

The introduction of the railways, in the second half of the nineteenth century, helped to bring prosperity and modernity to the Irish countryside. By 1855, the main lines between Dublin and Belfast, Cork, Galway, Limerick and Waterford had been completed and a total of one thousand miles of rail had been laid. By 1865, this figure had doubled. By the railways' peak in 1920, Ireland had 3,400 miles of track. The new railways cut the time and cost of travel in half. They also put an end to the passenger traffic on the canals and made mail coaches obsolete.

The railways provided employment to the rural population through their construction and operation. Ordinary people became much more mobile and could travel greater distances than ever before. Farmers also benefited from the new mode of transport, because cattle could be easily transported from the remoter areas to the ports for export. As a result, the railways accelerated the changeover from tillage to pasture. They also helped the growth and development of market towns, particularly those that had cattle fairs.

The railways opened up the countryside to the market economy, providing a variety of consumer goods, and the railways facilitated the tourism industry, with new hotels being built to cater for travellers in holiday resorts such as Killarney, Sligo and Kilkee. The railways also increased the rate of emigration, however. Impoverished farmers were only a train ticket from the emigration boat. Local trades were exposed to competition from Dublin, local industries were forced to compete with imported goods, and many small industries in the provinces were forced to shut down.

Once the railways were built, the great fair in Ballinasloe started to go down gradually, as a number of new fairs started up. It was understandable that people travelling from Mayo wondered why they couldn't have a fair in their local area, and it was the same for the people from the far side of Galway and the people from Roscommon. So fairs were started in Tuam in Galway, Boyle in Roscommon, and Moate in Westmeath. My father was very fond of going to the fair in Balla in County Mayo, which had cattle from Leitrim, Sligo, Galway and the Belmullet peninsula.

Other fairs started up in Munster: in south Tipperary, Limerick and west Clare. It was always said that a thousand cows came into the parish of Ratoath after the fair in Ennistymon, County Clare, which took place every year on 25 March. Ratoath was a great area in Meath for feeding these cows, as was the land around Dunboyne, Kilbride and Clonee.

Back in those days, there were men who were known as 'tanglers', who attended fairs to make bargains. These men had very little money outside of the money they earned at fairs, and they wanted to save as much of that money as possible.

They had all kinds of tricks for travelling free on the train. One was to find an old ticket and to chew the date off. When the checker came to check the tickets, the man would start to search all of his pockets, up and down, down and up. Finally the checker would say to him, 'Ah look, isn't that it you have in your mouth'. The tangler would say, 'Ah, bedad, I never realised that's where I left it', and because it was chewed it was hard to check.

On one occasion, my father was travelling down on the train to a fair in the south of Ireland. Now, you can quite understand that men of a similar background would travel together in the carriage so that they could talk and read if they wanted, and not be annoyed by people of a different kind, who would have very different ideas about various matters.

The carriage was full leaving Kingsbridge, but after the tickets had been checked, they heard a shuffling under the seat. They moved their legs and a small man came out from underneath. He was a tramp or a drover and he didn't have the price of a ticket. He found a small bit of room on a seat and announced that he would sit there until they got to the next station, where the tickets would be checked again. There were no corridors on those trains, so the tickets couldn't be checked unless the train was stopped in a station, with a checker opening the door of each carriage.

'When we get to the next station, I'll disappear under the seat and let none of you mention anything about me', he said. So they told him that, of course, they wouldn't mention a thing. Then he looked at them and was able to tell each one of them some peculiarity about themselves, with regards to the fairs, to what they would do and what they would say. These things were perfectly true, but I don't suppose they cared to hear them.

'Ah Mister Ward! Always divides the five shillings when he's buying a cow,' he said, which I suppose is correct.

Then he looked at Mister Kennedy of Straffan, who regarded himself as being rather grand. He had very little money, but he had a lot of land, which he stocked with small heifers and low-priced old cows. He used to sell the heifers over in Manchester and would say to the butchers or wholesale men over there, 'These are all cake-fed heifers'.

The man from under the seat started to take off Kennedy's high-pitched Anglo-Irish voice, and he took him off very well.

'Mister Kennedy and his cake-fed heifers,' he said. 'He hasn't cake for himself, let alone for the cattle.'

Which, of course, was quite true. Kennedy drew himself up as high as he could and put up with the remark, which everybody else knew was correct. Then the drover mentioned another man who had to borrow money from a firm called Gavin Lowe's in order to buy any cattle, because he had next to no money. It all goes to show that the man knew what was going on.

These men were very uneducated and had been kept down by very bad landlords. I suppose that's why they were inclined to take it out on anybody they came up against. On one occasion in Nenagh my father refused to take a cow from a tangler. The tangler would have bought it a few hours before with the idea of selling it on for another five or ten shillings. My father didn't see why he should part with five or ten shillings to this man and he refused to take the cow. The tangler said to him, 'Some day, when you're not looking and are getting into a railway carriage, I'll cut you in two with an ash plant.' They used to carry heavy sticks cut from an ash tree.

He would have, too, because they were very lawless. Those men had very little to lose and if he got three or six months in jail, he'd be better kept and better fed than he would have been at home.

My father always made it his business to be off the streets of Nenagh, County Tipperary, before one o'clock in the afternoon, because the faction fights usually started around then. From one until late in the evenings, there was terrific fighting in the streets. In Nenagh, it was between a faction called the 'three-year-olds' and the 'four-year-olds'. Several people would be badly injured and beaten up on each side, and the causes of the rows were really unknown.

My father also used to go to Cappawhite in Tipperary, which had a frightfully lawless crowd in it. It's a place that you don't hear of now, but it's up in the mountains, and my father said that they came in once a year for the fair. They were rough and when they took poitín – which they did – it left them in a terrible humour.

There was no accommodation at these fairs, particularly at the fairs in the south. In those times, there would have been very little commercial traffic or anything of that kind – there might only be one hotel, of sorts.

When you arrived at the station in the town where the fair was to be held, those who had a bed booked walked slowly to their accommodation. The other people ran. The better-off people carried an umbrella and a leather bag. The bag contained boots, a spare cap and night clothes. The less well-off carried an ash plant and a brown paper parcel, which contained a night shirt. The underprivileged carried nothing but an ash plant.

The booking system was also unreliable. You could write to the hotel well before the date yet find that, when you arrived, somebody else had taken your bed, and you'd have to go around looking for another place.

My father often told stories about the various places he stopped in. He said that he used to look into the cupboards and under the beds before going asleep because he never knew what he would find. On one occasion, he heard a terrible squealing from the headboard of his bed. He got up to have a look and found that a cat had become wedged behind the headboard. On another occasion, he found plumes and a coffin under the bed and assumed that somebody in the house was expected to die.

Another time, he was stopping in a public house in Templemore, County Tipperary. It would often be very hard to get people to call you in the morning. In some cases the owners or porters took too much drink the night before and they didn't wake up, so you had to call yourself.

The buyers had to be up early, because the fairs started at dawn, even though the Wards never bought cattle until there was proper light. Some dealers carried lamps around, looked over the animal's back and bought it. It wasn't a good idea because sometimes they'd be lame or blind and then there'd be rows afterwards when the animals were seen in proper light.

On this particular occasion in Templemore, the pub owner didn't call him and father got up and came downstairs. He met the owner at the foot of the stairs.

'Ah! I didn't think you'd be getting up so soon. I was going up to call you to make you a cup of tea,' he said. 'I'm just busy here making whiskey for the fair men. They'll be in any time for it and I want to have it ready for them.'

He had two big tubs in the hall at the end of the stairs, with whiskey in one and water in the other. He had a bucket and he took a bucket of whiskey and threw it into the water and back and forth like that. He also had a sweeping brush to stir the two tubs together. When he was finished, he said, 'I'll make a cup of tea for you now.'

Those fellows, when they'd come in, would have been on the road from ten o'clock the night before, walking in with the cattle. They'd be desperate anxious for a drink and this strong stuff warmed them up well and they'd be in great form after taking it.

My father knew one man, Joe McLaughlin, who was a 'blocker'. This meant that he might buy a beast on its way into the fair for £11. Then he would sell it to somebody else for £11.10 and put the ten shillings in his pocket. If he got a few pounds for his day's work, then he was well satisfied.

McLaughlin carried his money in a bag, which he kept next to his shirt and which was tied around his waist with a belt or a cord. On a given date each year he counted the money in the bag, or asked somebody else to count it for him. If, at the end of the year, he had more money than he had upon the last counting, then it had been a good year for him. If he had less money, then he hoped that the next year would be better.

Joe was an over-zealous northern Catholic and carried on his person a number of small bottles of oil and a small tin of paste. Each night he anointed himself before he went to bed. This may have been a very good exercise to perform on himself. However, he also used to insist that whoever else was in the room with him be anointed also.

Mattie Ward of Bracetown (who was not related to us but worked at Gunnocks) spent a night in a room with McLaughlin and was told that he would have to be anointed. Mattie told him that he was not going to die, but his protests were of no avail. For the sake of peace, he let Joe anoint him. Joe also pinned a number of medals on Matt's clothes and hung several small pictures on the wall of the room.

The late Joe Coleman of Kilcock once gave McLaughlin a severe talking to for lighting all the candles in the stand in the church in Naas without putting one penny into the box.

On another occasion, my father was staying in a house in the square in Roscommon town. Joe came in and was given bed and breakfast, for which he used to pay three shillings. He did not know that the house had changed hands and that the woman had increased the charge to ten shillings. The next day he offered her three shillings, but she insisted on ten shillings. Joe paid, but around fifteen minutes later came down the stairs carrying the mattress on his back with the bedclothes wrapped up in it. He was halfway down the street when the woman's husband overtook him. He asked for the return of the bedclothes and McLaughlin said, 'Sure, didn't I buy my bed and I am taking it with me.' The man handed McLaughlin back the ten shillings and recovered the bedclothes.

Father was in Guy's Hotel in Tuam one March when the weather was very cold. After coming in on the late train, he went up to his room. He felt the blankets on the bed, which had been washed and washed until there was hardly a bit of wool left in them. That wasn't unusual: typically you'd sleep in your clothes to try to keep warm. But in this case there was almost nothing on the bed and he went down and asked for an extra blanket for the bed.

The porter told him that the house was full and there wasn't a blanket of any kind available, but he showed up a few minutes later and gave my father a tablecloth, which he used that night.

The following morning, there was a great deal of comment when the men went down to breakfast. They wondered why one table was without a tablecloth, but father kept quiet about it because he'd had the use of it for the night.

Another time he was in Mitchelstown and, after trying to find accommodation in a number of places, he was offered a bed in a half-loft. Half-lofts were built over one half of the kitchen and a bed was put in there. You had a ladder to climb from the kitchen into the loft. They were very warm and comfortable for the family, because you were directly above the heat of the kitchen. That was all very well if you were a member of the family, but my father was a very strict type of a man and he didn't like the idea of people below laughing and talking. They could also see him taking off his clothes – if he took them off.

Many of these places were dreadfully dirty places. Laurence stayed in a place in Rathkeale in County Limerick with Willie Yourell, who lived down near Trenchyard, and both of them got the most frightful colds out of it, absolutely dreadful. The beds were damp because the sheets and blankets were never changed on them and they were left made up all year round. They were in bed for several weeks with frightful colds because of the dirty conditions.

Mister Ludlow's in Loughrea was an exception: Mister Ludlow was a north-of-Ireland man who was a sub-agent to the Clancarthy estate in Galway. He only put up six people in the house and they had to be of very good character. It was excellently well run.

I went with my father to Loughrea when I was a boy and I was very impressed when it came to serving the dinner. A joint of mutton was put on the table for us and as soon as the six or seven people were given their dinner, Mister Ludlow started to give us a sermon. It was chiefly about the Man Above; he read extracts from the Bible and spoke to us about it. I don't know what particular brand of religion he was, but whatever about the religion; the food, the bed and the place was excellent.

The fair at Spancil Hill, County Clare took place around three miles from Ennis and it was the earliest fair in the country. When I say early, I mean early in the morning, because it took place on 21 June, the longest day of the year.

The fair was held at a crossroads: there was no house of any kind, not even a public house. There was nothing but the field and the four roads and the cattle – nearly all cows – that were collected there. You would be standing on the hill, waiting for the cattle to come in, when the sun was coming up at one in the morning.

On one occasion, my father was at Spancil Hill, chatting with some of the Cuffes, a number of the Frosts and a well-known cattle man called Tom Crowe. The Wards were cousins of the Cuffes and one or two of the Cuffes were married to Frosts. The Cuffes used to buy a lot of their cattle in Clare and also sold cattle for their Clare customers in Dublin. The Frosts were a great Clare family: they were originally from Wales, but had big estates around Sixmilebridge, Cratlow and Ennis.

They were chatting close to an encampment of tinkers by the fair green. Nowadays they're called itinerants, but up to comparatively recently they were always called tinkers, for the very simple reason that they were tinsmiths, mending kettles and pans and all of that kind of thing.

A woman came out of one of the tents, carrying a baby. Her husband was outside shouting abuse and went to attack her. She was a great big woman and she held the baby in one arm and boxed her husband with the other arm. Any time he tried to get a blow at her with his fists, she held the baby out in front. Because he didn't want to hit the baby, he missed her and she hit him every time. After seven or eight severe blows to the head, he hoofed it and ran off.

In the south of Ireland, you had what were known as 'cow doctors'. You wouldn't find these men in the west of Ireland. These cow doctors were well-known men who would buy an unhealthy cow – a delicate cow – and dose her with various herbal cures, because there were no patent medicines at that time.

They also doctored them in other ways, by buying an old cow with a good figure and making her look young. Nowadays all cows are pollys – hornless – but in those days all cows had horns. The cow doctors filed the cow's horns and rubbed pipe clay – which was like chalk – into the horn to make it white. That wouldn't do, because they'd be too white – people would know that there was something wrong with her. So they rubbed ordinary clay into it to make it look natural, so that she had no rings to show her age. So there she was, a smart, young-looking cow stepping out.

The problem was that she would only have had a few teeth, if she had any teeth at all. If you were a bit doubtful about a cow, then you caught her to look at her teeth. The cow doctors forestalled that kind of action by giving her a tip with a red-hot iron on the nose before she was brought into the fair. The moment you tried to catch her, you wouldn't get any way near her at all. So if you bought her, you were taking a chance, and some people did.

These fairs in the south of Ireland were attended by a number of north-of-Ireland men. My father used to talk about one very well-known man, Johnny Johnson from Ballybay, County Monaghan, whose son I knew. Johnson used to buy around 150 cows in the fair in Templemore, and he'd buy the best cows in the fair. I don't know how much they would have cost, maybe £6 or £8 or £10 each. Twelve pounds is the most you would have paid at that time.

All of the cows Johnson bought were in lots of one or two, each of which was paid for in cash. The cattle men paid for the cows with the notes they kept in their pockets. The usual thing at that time was to get a shilling back from the seller for 'luck' – which was really quite a good deal.

I know from experience that it's very difficult to pay a large number of men. Sometimes, I would have to pay as many as twenty, and they would all push around you, saying, 'Pay me, pay me next, here boss, I'm on the road since twelve last night and I didn't get any breakfast', and all of this kind of thing. They'd be pushing and pulling at you, and it was quite difficult to satisfy them.

One day in Templemore, Johnny Johnson saw a man with a horse and creel, which he would have used for carrying pigs or sheep. He borrowed it, sat in it, and paid one hundred men for one hundred and fifty cattle, over the side of the creel.

Other men would have a big hat and they'd keep the money in the hat. If there were two men conducting the business, two brothers perhaps, one would hold the hat while the other would pay out of it.

My father knew two northern tanglers, by the names of Doran and McMahon. These men were partners and would buy twenty or more cattle in a lot and resell them at the same fair.

At one particular fair in Moate, County Westmeath, my father was very surprised to meet McMahon, dressed as a parson. He knew that both Doran and McMahon were Catholics. McMahon got into a conversation with a Protestant farmer, who had a number of cattle to sell.

McMahon told the farmer that he was collecting money for his poor boy's home in the north of Ireland. He also told him that he knew a cattle buyer who was 'the right sort' and would give him a good price for his cattle.

Doran was brought along, negotiations began, and the parson said 'divide' [presumably 'split the difference'] on several occasions. After some time, the farmer sold his cattle to Doran, who gave McMahon a pound for his school. The farmer, not to be outdone, also gave him a pound. In the end, Doran and McMahon bought some very cheap cattle.

You had all kinds of people at fairs. During one particular period, a black man – I assume he was an American Negro – used to attend the fairs in order to extract teeth. He carried out the extractions in public, on a stand in the street, with maybe one hundred or more people looking on to see what was happening. If anybody in the audience had trouble with one of their teeth, then they would stand in line to climb up on the stand, where this – no doubt very experienced – man would pull their teeth.

He brought with him a number of other coloured men, who had brass instruments, and they played and made any amount of noise on the brass instruments while the people's teeth were being extracted. The idea was that, if the person shouted out in pain when the tooth was being pulled, the band was making so much noise that the next person in line wouldn't be able to hear them, so the band played the whole time.

The fairs in west Clare – in Tulla, Ennistymon, Kilfenora and Kilmihil – were known as 'walking fairs', because the cattle that were bought at it had to be walked a considerable distance to the railway stations in Birdhill and Killaloe. They were taken in cattle wagons to Hazelhatch and walked from there to Gunnocks, Ratoath and County Dublin.

Father used to bring a man with him to walk the cows to the station. He usually brought one of the Earley or Phoenix family with him, since they would look after the cows better than a hired drover. He would also hire another man at the fair to help, and maybe a second man if you were driving cows.

Anybody who knows anything about cows knows that they know their own home place, because they've been there for years and have been well minded and looked after by the people in that place. So when they were taken to a fair, their whole anxiety was to get home as quickly as possible. This only applies to cows; it doesn't apply to bullocks and heifers.

Cows were very difficult to drive until they got tired. When you started to walk them towards Killaloe, they instinctively knew the direction they came from and the direction they were going in. Let's say you had twenty-seven cows, which would fill three wagons. If five or six of them got away from the others, they'd go up side roads or they'd go up crossroads. The ones that came from the far side of the town tried to go back into the town, because they knew what direction they had come from. There was hardly a time or a fair that you wouldn't lose some of them, either before you got them to the railway station, or when you took them off the train. The same carry-on began when they got off the train: they wanted to get back home again, and they ran in all directions.

It often happened that they got to the station and found that they were short one or two of their cows, so one of them had to go back and find them. You couldn't go back to the seller, because you wouldn't have had his address if you only bought one or two cows.

So they went to the schoolhouse and asked permission from the schoolmaster to tell the children about the missing cows. The children were delighted and they'd be on the lookout for a cow, or they'd know Pat Murphy or John Daly or whoever had sold the cow, and you'd be able to get in touch with him, and that's how you'd find the cows.

The cows could be missing for a fortnight or three weeks, and then you'd have to wait for another fair in the district so that there would be a train coming up. Then you'd have to buy a few more cows to go along with the ones you'd lost. Then you could lose one or two out of that lot. It was very troublesome, so they would really want to buy animals that were worth the money, with all of the bother that was attached to them.

Kit McCormack, who lived in Elickstown, Dunboyne, used to walk his cattle from Maam Cross in Connemara to Dunboyne. These were six-and seven-year-old bullocks off the mountains, and the walk did not upset them in any way. When the farmer was making a deal for the cattle, the herds were not allowed to hear the price. If it got to be known that a farmer had got more for his cattle than his neighbour, the herds would start to fight with each other with sticks. It was not unusual for one or two to be killed, because they took a great interest in their employers' animals.

My father also used to buy around thirty Galloway bullocks from the Coneys brothers, from Clifden, in the May Fair in Galway. These bullocks were shod with 'plates', so that if they didn't sell they could walk them home again. As soon as the bullocks were sold, the herds took the 'plates' off and kept them for the following year. However, in one particular year, the deal was not made and the herds refused to drive the bullocks home, because their own boots were so bad. At that point, the Coneys brothers had to negotiate with their own men to bring the bullocks home.

When the cows arrived at Gunnocks, some of them wouldn't have 'dried off': they would still have been producing milk. So you took milk from them once a week and after two or three weeks they dried up completely.

To prevent them from getting mastitis, they made a solution of Archangel tar and train oil and applied it with a little home-made thing that looked like a cricket bat. It kept the flies off, there was no doubt about that. It sealed the top of the teat and the flies wouldn't go near it because of the smell and the stickiness of it.

Friday was the day for tarring the cows at my Uncle Michael's place in Kilcloon. After the first or second tarring, it was practically impossible to get the cows into the pen, because the tar used to burn. They'd disappear into the ditches and everywhere, after that stuff was put on them. They got to know Fridays, after the first three or four times, and you'd have to beat them out of the ditches, because they'd go in early to avoid being brought into the yard.

My uncle used to recruit a lot of children from the school beside his farm. In those days, it didn't really matter very much whether the children missed out on a day of school, or two or three days for that matter, if there was anything better to be done.

He was a very generous class of a man and he gave them sixpence for the day, which was very good because he liked having them, so he'd get a whole army of children. I remember them myself, the noise of them. They'd round up the cows and get them into the yard.

He'd have a hundred and fifty cows to do on a Friday, and they'd tar them there and then, and let them all out again. You wouldn't see them for the smoke going out of the yard. The tarring continued through most of the summer until around the first week in September, when the flies were gone.

5

Laurence Ward,

Member of the Grand Jury

My father was on the Grand Jury of County Meath, was a justice of the peace, was a member of the Dunshaughlin Board of Guardians, and was the chairman of the Rural District Council. All of those things were use-ful to have – from the nationalist point of view – because the majorities on these boards were pro-British.

As a Justice of the Peace, Laurence was something like a present-day district-court judge. He sat on the Bench in Dunshaughlin perhaps once per month, and heard and adjudicated the different small cases that came up.

He was also the chairman of the Dunshaughlin Union – the work-house – for many years. He did all he could to improve the food and con-ditions for the poor people in it. He was instrumental in building the long row of two-storey houses that runs along one side of Avondale Terrace, opposite Saint Peter's Park, in Dunboyne.

My father was the second Catholic Grand Jurer in Meath. The first one was P. J. Kennedy, of Rathgore House in Enfield, who was also a member of parliament for County Meath.

It was Kennedy who got my father onto the Grand Jury of County Meath, which was exclusively Protestant and pro-British as well. I have one letter here in front of me:

February 23, 1910
From the office at Kells.

I have to inform you that the Grand Jury of County Meath will be called and sworn for the discharge of crown business at the opening of the commission at 11.30 am on Monday, February 28, 1910 at the courthouse in Trim. I trust it may be convenient for you to attend.

I am, dear sir, yours faithfully

P. J. Kennedy.

To Laurence Ward, JP.

The Grand Jury was a very difficult position for Catholics to attain, and quite a number of people didn't approve of him being elected to it, because he was of a nationalist outlook. The Grand Jury looked after local justice and civil administration.

The Protestants held on to as many grand jury-ships as they could and resisted my father getting on to the grand jury. When he did get on, he was not liked by the other members, and they kept him off committees as much as they possibly could. However, he was a very determined sort of man and was not going to be beaten down.

One of the other justices of the peace and grand jurors from around this area was a man called 'Fisty' Butler, who lived in Priestown, Kilbride. I don't know his Christian name; I never heard it. He was always called Fisty because he had only one arm.

His arm was damaged in an accident and he was brought to Dublin to have it taken off. Before the operation took place, he said to the surgeon, 'I want you to put that arm to one side for me, because I will bring it home and bury it in Kilbride graveyard, where I hope to be buried myself at a later date. After all,' he said, 'I don't want to be going into heaven with only one arm.'

The arm was parcelled up; he brought it home and buried it in Kilbride graveyard.

Butler and my father got on very well. They used to travel in the same railway carriage to fairs in the south of Ireland in the spring. They were both very fond of going to Cappawhite in south Tipperary, which is up in the hills and was a notorious place for faction fights.

Although Butler had a big holding, he didn't dress expensively. My father remembered travelling with him one day and noticing that he had a hole in the knee of his trousers. Whoever was sitting opposite them kept putting their finger into the hole, and Butler didn't like the idea of people drawing attention to it.

He used to get a very cheap holiday every year; staying with his brother, who was an Anglican clergyman in Wiesbaden, in Germany. At that time people used to go there to take the waters, and his brother ministered to the English-speaking tourists that visited the city.

Even though Butler had only one arm, he was a very good shot. There were a lot of crows in the rookery at Priestown. He was very keen on fox-hunting, so he shot the crows and threw them into the foxes' dens to feed the foxes. When he went fox-hunting on horseback, he held the reins in his teeth and held on to the pummel of the saddle with one hand.

He had a big place with a lot of outhouses and he kept his yard very well. A lot of the maintenance was carried out by an excellent carpenter called Larry Gerrity, who lived at Nuttstown.

Butler kept a pet monkey, who discovered that Larry used to keep his lunch in the pocket of his coat, which was hung in the house. On more than one occasion, the monkey ate the lunch before Larry got to it.

On another occasion, the monkey took Larry Gerrity's ruler. In those days, wages were low and rulers cost a fair bit, so Larry tried to coax the monkey to give him back the ruler. The monkey wouldn't give it back and ran up to the top of one of the outhouses. Larry got a ladder and climbed up after the monkey. The monkey kept moving away from him, and Larry kept trying to coax him. Finally – as a concession to Larry – the monkey started breaking bits off the ruler and throwing them to Larry. The ruler wasn't much use after that.

There is one story about Fisty Butler that has a connection with Norman's Grove. Back around 1890, an elderly gentleman called Shanley called on Andrew Clarke, who owned a pub in Clonee. Shanley told Clarke that a regiment of British soldiers would be passing through the village on their way to manoeuvres near Navan and would require refreshments and a rest. The gentleman told Clarke that if he supplied them with drinks, the British army would pay Clarke.

Clarke agreed to do so, and the man then asked Clarke for ten pounds. The money was either a short-term loan, or was demanded as a consideration for providing the business. Shanley made the same arrangement with a publican in Dunshaughlin and collected another sum of money. No soldiers came to Clonee on the appointed day, and Clarke did not see Shanley again until he was arrested and charged with getting money by false pretences. He was brought before the Grand Jury in Trim, where he came before both my father and Fisty Butler.

The prisoner stated that as a boy – around 1835 – he had lived in Norman's Grove. Father asked him to describe the house and lawns. He did so, and stated that he and his brothers had cut their names on the big beech trees in the front lawn. My father had often seen the name Shanley cut into the big beech trees in the woods opposite the house, and verified that a family of Shanleys had lived in Norman's Grove.

Butler then asked the man where he had gone to school. It happened that Fisty Butler had attended that school.

'Look, tell me this,' Fisty said to the man. 'How did the boys get out of the dormitory after lights-out?'

Shanley told Butler about a particular window at the end of the passage that they were able to open and climb through. Butler said that he was perfectly correct.

'There is no doubt,' he said. 'You are Shanley.'

The jury found him guilty, but they decided not to send him to jail. He was either cautioned or fined. Then the Grand Jury took up a collection among themselves, either to pay Shanley's fine, or to help out an old man who had seen better days.

Andrew Clarke's pub is now owned by Michael Dwyer, who calls it 'The Millhouse', because there used to be a water-driven flour grinding mill in the back yard. When Michael Dwyer was making the car park, he dug up two of the old mill wheels, which he placed against the end wall.

I have been asked many times whether the Ward family have always been Catholics. As far as I am aware, they always have. When I tell people this, I am immediately asked, 'How then did you hold so much good land?' I suppose the reason is that our landlords were themselves Catholics.

In 1570, part of Gunnocks had the Hollywood family as landlords and they were a Catholic family. In 1640, most of the lands were owned by Alderman Thomas Clarke, who lived in Dublin. The rest of the land was owned by Richard Plunkett of Dunshaughlin, a member of the Fingal family, who owned Dunsoghly Castle near Dublin Airport. When Plunkett signed old deeds, he wrote 'Richard Plunkett de Gunockes'. He was a cousin of St Oliver Plunkett.

The Corballis family was another Catholic landlord family in the area. They lived in Ratoath Manor, which is now a nursing home for elderly ladies.

The Irish National League
Union is Strength

Laurence Ward
Was admitted a member of Dunboyne Branch
This 17th Day of March 1886
John Rooney, Honorary Secretary, No. 4191

Objects of the League
The Irish National Land League was formed for the following objects:
First – To put an end to rack-renting, eviction and Landlord oppression.
Second – To effect such radical change in the land system of Ireland as will put it in the power of every Irish farmer to become the owner, on fair terms, of the land he tills.
The means proposed to effect these objects are:
(1) Organisation among the people and tenant farmers for the purpose of self-defence and inculcating the absolute necessity of their refusing to take any farm from which another may be evicted, or from purchasing any cattle or goods which many be seized on for non-payment of impossible rent.
(2) The cultivation of public opinion by persistent exposure, in the press and by public meetings, of the monstrous injustice of the present system and of its ruinous results
(3) A resolute demand for the reduction of the excessive rents which have brought the Irish people to a state of starvation.
(4) Temperate but firm resistance to oppression and injustice.

Our properties in Whitestown and Fieldstown were rented from the Eyre Cootes, a Protestant Cromwellian family who settled in Laois. They were good landlords and you may take it that the Wards were good tenants. The Eyre Cootes were on good terms with my father and with Laurence of Fieldstown and would call up to see them even up to the end of the Second World War.

One twenty-one-acre field in the middle of Gunnocks – known as Bowdeens – was owned by the Lewis family, who lived near Mullingar and owned a lot of land in Westmeath. As far as I know, it was the only bit of land that the Lewis family owned in this part of the country, apart from a plot at the back of a house in Clonee.

The holder of the Lewis estate died with no obvious heir, so the trustees had to look for the next of kin. It turned out to be an old cabman who had his stand along the railings of Trinity College Dublin. When asked to come to the Four Courts to signs the papers and inherit the estate, he replied, 'I am all my life sitting on this old cab and I will not get down to sign any papers.'

However, his daughter, Jane Isabella, was made of sterner stuff. She signed the papers and became the owner of the Lewis estate.

It was always the policy of the Ward Family to pay the rents directly to the landlords, rather than paying through an agent. When Jane Isabella Lewis inherited the estate, father wrote to her, informing her that he would pay the rent directly to her. She replied to his letter, agreeing to this arrangement. By this point, she had moved away from the Coombe, where she was originally from, and the return address was 'Jane Isabella Lewis, Villa Isabella, Monte Carlo, France'. It was a rags-to-riches story.

My father also used to pay two shillings and sixpence annual rent for a three-acre field near Gunnocks. The rent was sent to a parson who was living in County Wexford. It was common for someone to rent land from a landlord but the tithes for it maybe went to a clergyman or a family who were not necessarily connected to the landlord.

On one occasion, my father read the demand note and realised that it demanded rent for 'your land in Kilbride'. However, all of my father's land was in Dunboyne parish, so he sent back a letter saying that he had no land in Kilbride, but that if the parson could tell him where it was, he would be glad to pay him the two and sixpence.

'But until you are able to tell me where the land is, I will not pay two and sixpence to you any more.'

My father didn't object to paying the rent, but to the annoyance of going to the post office twice a year to get a postal order for one shilling and threepence.

There were one or two solicitor's letters from the parson, but they were unable to prove that my father had land in Kilbride, so the payments stopped.

Between 1879 and 1909, Irish farmers wrested control, and ultimately ownership, of their farms from the landlords. Michael Davitt started the mass movement which resulted in this massive social and economic reform, which still defines land-ownership patterns in Ireland today.

Michael Davitt was born in County Mayo in 1846, at the height of the Great Famine. When he was six years old, the seven members of his family were evicted from their home and moved to Lancashire, England. Davitt began work in a factory at the age of nine, but soon lost an arm in an industrial accident.

After his injury, he was able to focus on his education and found a job as an errand boy and later as a bookkeeper. He took night classes and was particularly interested in Irish history and politics.

In 1865, Davitt joined a secret revolutionary group, the Irish Republican Brotherhood, known as the Fenians. His activities included recruiting members and smuggling arms into Ireland. He was arrested in 1870 and jailed for treason, serving seven years of his fifteen-year sentence.

Upon his release, he decided to campaign for land reform in Ireland, believing that the land of Ireland should belong to the people of the country rather than to a handful of landlords, many of whom lived in England.

In 1879, he was a key founder of the Irish National Land League, which was set up to campaign for tenants' rights. The organisation campaigned for three years, until it achieved the 'Three Fs' for Irish tenants: fair rent, fixity of tenure, and free sale of the tenant's equitable interest in their farm.

The League organised resistance to evictions, reductions in rents, and relief for evicted families. The Land League famously organised the ostracism of Captain Charles Boycott, a County Mayo land agent, in the autumn of 1880. Boycott ultimately had to leave Ireland, and the incident led to the coining of the term 'boycott'.

In 1882, Davitt was elected Member of Parliament for County Meath. He started to campaign for land nationalisation and an alliance between the British working class, Irish labourers and tenant farmers. This political and social agenda alienated many farmers, who were more conservative in outlook.

In 1890, he initiated the Irish Democratic Labour Federation, an organisation which campaigned for free education, worker housing, reduced working hours, universal suffrage and land nationalisation.

When Davitt died in 1906, more than twenty thousand people attended his funeral, including the Lord Lieutenant of Ireland. He is regarded as one of the founders of the British Labour Party. Mahatma Gandhi attributed the origin of his own mass movement of peaceful resistance in India to Davitt and the Land League.

My father used to buy a large number of cows in Clare in the springtime of the year. County Clare – at the time I'm talking about – was probably the most disturbed county in Ireland. There was a lot of agrarian trouble and the number of shootings and burnings in Clare was legion. It was a place with a lot of big estates, many evictions, and quite a number of bad landlords.

Father used to stay in a hotel, and would take an outside car out to wherever the fair was taking place, whether it was Kilmeaden, Spancil Hill, Ennistymon or Scariff. He would share the expense of the car with two or more people.

'Ah sure, you remember so-and-so?' the driver would say to them. 'Well now, he was shot there from behind that bush.'

Then you'd go on to some other place and he'd say, 'Do you remember so-and-so?'

'Oh yes, I do.'

'Well, he was shot from behind that wall,' he'd relay. 'That was so-and-so's place up there, and it was burned down.'

As a boy, I remember twenty particular cattle grazing in the big field in Paceland. 'Those are the last of Frank Shawe Taylor's cattle', my father told me. They were the worst of his cattle, but they were really magnificent cattle. One particular black horny bullock sticks out in my mind, a magnificent beast.

Frank Shawe Taylor had a huge amount of land, around Loughrea and Gort. The local people would have been happy if he had agreed to give three or four farms to them, but he was a very determined sort of a man. The only way he would give up land was if it was given to ex-soldiers, who had fought in the First World War. That did not go down well with the local people, and he wouldn't agree to anything else, so they decided to shoot him.

Frank Shawe Taylor – he was always called Frank, because his full name was too long – was to be shot on his way to Athenry. It would be dark and he would be travelling on an outside car – a type of horse carriage.

He had a man named Bermingham, a local farmer who was very popular in the area. He used to help Frank and went with him to the various fairs in the area. The night before, some of the boys called to

Bermingham's house and told him that when Frank called for him at five o'clock in the morning, he was not to go in the car. He was to give the excuse that he was sick. He wondered why he was not to go with Frank, but they said that they were telling him what to do.

'You're to say that you're sick, that you're sorry, but that you can't go with him.'

Bermingham suspected what was going to happen, but he didn't want to be shot himself. When Frank called to him that morning, he came out and said that he was very sick, that he had a very heavy cold and that he was sorry but that he wouldn't be going with him. Within half an hour, Frank had been shot. It was a hard decision for Birmingham to make, especially as he couldn't tell Frank that he suspected that he was going to be shot.

Frank's land was divided up by the Irish Land Commission and the Congested Districts Board after his death, and Laurence of Fieldstown bought the last twenty of his five hundred bullocks. After the land had been divided, my father met one of the old herds in Ballinasloe. The herd was selling a few cattle, and Laurence said to the herd, 'Wasn't it a terrible thing to shoot Mister Shawe Taylor.'

'Ah, look here, Mister Ward,' the herd said. 'It has done a great deal of good already; half a dozen farms have been divided up and they're going to divide the rest of them.'

I know Laurence didn't expect that answer and he certainly did not approve of the sentiments behind it.

The first Irish Land Act was introduced by the Liberal Prime Minister, William Gladstone, in 1870, as part of his mission to pacify Ireland. It attempted to provide legal protection to tenants by providing rent control and tenure rights. It also included a measure whereby the British government would loan money to tenants to buy their holdings, but only if the landlord agreed to sell.

In practice it was a very weak act, but it was significant because it indicated that the British government was prepared to get involved in landlord-tenant relations, overruling the 'laissez-faire' principal that landlords were entitled to do as they wished with their private property.

The Second Irish Land Act, introduced by Gladstone in 1881, granted fair rent and fixity of tenure, and gave tenants a legal right to sell any improvements they had made on their farm, if they chose to move on – a right known as 'freedom of sale'. These reform measures were to be overseen by a new government body, the Irish Land Commission. After the introduction of this Act, Charles Stuart Parnell lost interest in the issue of land reform and focused on the issue of Home Rule for Ireland.

In September 1902, Captain John Shawe-Taylor, the son of a County Galway landlord, called for a conference between representatives of Irish landlords and tenants to settle the long dispute over land tenure. Many landlords, trapped in a cycle of eroded rents and diminished rights over their own property, were attracted by the idea of selling their estates to their tenants.

The Chief Secretary for Ireland – George Wyndham – gave his backing to a Land Conference in December 1902, comprising four landlord representatives and four tenant representatives. They worked out a new scheme for tenant land purchase, based on the idea that the British government would pay the difference between the price offered by tenants and that demanded by landlords.

The Land Purchase Act of 1903, known as 'The Wyndham Act', finished off landlordism, by making it easier for tenants to purchase land, and facilitated the transfer of about nine million acres by 1914. In 1909, the Birrell Act made it compulsory for landlords to sell their estates to their tenants.

It is often forgotten that the bulk of Irish farmers obtained ownership of their holdings as a result of legislation introduced by a British Conservative Party government. Although the powers of the Irish Land Commission became far stronger under the Irish Free State, the bulk of the land-ownership transfer took place prior to the establishment of the Irish State.

The British government's motivation for this reform was largely political. The Conservatives wanted to end the government's massive involvement in the land market by ending the 'Three Fs' scheme. By forcing the landlords to sell to their tenants, they hoped to create a large, conservative, land-owning middle class in Ireland. They also hoped to convince Irish farmers that their economic interests would be better served within the United Kingdom than they would be under Home Rule.

The Land Purchase Acts did not achieve the aims of Michael Davitt, who sought nationalisation of the land of Ireland, rather than its transfer into the hands of just three hundred thousand private individuals.

During the Land Wars, a Scottish man by the name of Aries Mather took possession of a vast area of very bad land, between Athlone and Torcmaconnell, County Westmeath, and down to Mealig, in east Galway. He evicted a large number of tenants, but he also gave a lot of employment. He started a sawmill; he improved the land by draining it and cutting the scrub; he took down stone walls and filled in hollows.

Nevertheless, people preferred to keep their small subsistence holdings, rather than be evicted and take a job on the estate. Aries Mather became terribly unpopular and was always guarded by the military with guns.

He was a marked man. When he brought his cattle into the fair in Ballinasloe, he was escorted by armed police, who protected him and his cattle. On one occasion my father came out of a house where Mather was staying and found that the local people had dug a big hole outside the house. They said that they were digging a grave for Mather. It was not at all unusual to dig graves outside the houses of people who had taken possession of land or who had evicted the tenants or anything of that kind. Mather didn't need any warnings; he'd been warned plenty of times before.

It goes without saying that neither my father, nor my uncles, nor Laurence of Fieldstown would go near Mather's cattle; certainly none of the Ward family would buy cattle under those circumstances.

Licence for Arms (Except Revolver)
Granted upon Magistrates' Certificate under Section 4, Sub-Sec (4) of 'The
Peace Preservation (Ireland) Act, 1881.'
County of Meath, Petty Sessions District of Dunboyne

I, Thos. M French, being duly appointed and authorised in that behalf, do hereby grant to Laurence Ward, farmer, Norman's Grove, Clonee in pursuance of a Certificate dated the 9th day of January, 1882 and signed by J Hamilton, Esq and L Butler Esquire, being two Justices of the Peace for the said County and residing within the same Petty Sessions District as the said Laurence Ward in the County of Meath, that he is to their own personal knowledge a fit and proper person to have and carry one single shotgun and arm in the county of Meath.

Dated this 12th Day of January, 1882.

T. H. French

Note: This licence does not authorize having or carrying a Revolver and is in addition to and not in substitution for, any licence under 'The Gun Licence Act, 1870,' or 'The Explosives Act, 1875,' or which is otherwise by law required.

I once attended a funeral in County Limerick. As I entered the church, I remarked to a local man that the mass was likely to be over by half-twelve.

'I doubt it, said Croker' was his response. He was correct, because the mass wasn't over until one o'clock.

I know the origin of that saying. One of the huge estates in County Limerick, called Ballingarde, belonged to the Barrington family. It was comprised of thousands of acres of good land and has since been divided.

When Croker Barrington was dying, he was sitting at the window, looking out at his estate. The parson was trying to console him, and said, 'You are going to a far, far better land.'

'I doubt it,' said Croker. 'I doubt it.'

Once the Wyndham Act had been passed, the land-reform movement lost much of its momentum. As a result of the land reform, much of the best land in Leinster and Munster was now in the ownership of a relatively small number of Catholic nationalist farmers. The smaller farmers found little common cause with the bigger farmers, outside of their desire for Home Rule, and the land-reform movement splintered or faded away.

The United Irish League (UIL) was formed as a nationalist party in the aftermath of the Parnellite split in the Irish Parliamentary Party (IPP). Its founders included William O'Brien, Michael Davitt and John Dillon, and its political programme included agrarian agitation, political reform and Home Rule.

The leaders of this party had very different ideas about the priorities for the party. O'Brien was motivated by a wish to help small tenant farmers and landless labourers, particularly in the west of Ireland, who worked less fertile holdings. He championed the smallholders against the graziers, who owned large fertile farms and who raised cattle for export to England.

Davitt was more interested in state ownership and agrarian socialism and was not a believer in peasant proprietorship. John Dillon was primarily interested in Home Rule and opposed any land reform that drove a wedge between different sectors of nationalist Ireland.

The League's first electoral target was the first county-council elections, which took place in 1898. The UIL performed well and threatened the position of the IPP. It forced the pro-Parnell and anti-Parnell wings of the IPP to come together under the leadership of John Redmond, who led the party until the end of the First World War and who saw the introduction of the third and final Home Rule bill in Westminster.

The UIL merged with the IPP, operating as a constituency support organisation.

O'Brien was instrumental in the introduction of the Wyndham Land Act in 1903, which resulted in the sale of most estates to the tenant farmers.

After the Wyndham Act, small farmers and the graziers found little common cause on the land issue. In 1906, Laurence Ginnell, a Westmeath barrister, organised the Ranch War, which was supported by the UIL. The Ranch War aimed to secure better land for smallholders by deterring large-scale grazing, or 'ranching'. Its methods included boycotting, cattle-driving and occasional outbreaks of violence.

However, the leaders of the UIP included a large number of graziers, who sat on platforms denouncing the system from which they were profiting. The Ranch War lost momentum in 1909, but the political ideas that underlay it – that large-scale cattle grazing constituted a social injustice – continued as an important political idea into the 1940s.

There was a builder's providers strike in 1890, which may have been one of the first strikes in Dublin. The strike affected a wholesaler called Pyles, where my father used to get a lot of timber, nails, bolts, screws and that sort of thing.

Although the Pyles men were in a union, they had no funds and began to get hungry after a week or so. The foreman was a man called Larry Gerrity, who had no connection with the Larry Gerrity at Nuttstown. They just had the same name.

Larry Gerrity approached my father, who was living at Norman's Grove. Gerrity wanted Laurence to employ the striking workers, but wanted them to live at Norman's Grove, so that their employers would believe them to be on strike and would be forced to give in to their demands. Norman's Grove needed to be re-roofed, which would have been quite expensive, in terms of new timber, slate and labour. He agreed a price with Gerrity, with the understanding that Gerrity would settle with the men.

A large number of men came out to Norman's Grove and stripped off a large section of the roof. Then Gerrity came back to my father and said that the men were not happy with what had been agreed and that he would have to pay him more money.

Father refused to pay more, saying that he would pay the amount agreed and no more.

'They're after stripping half the roof, what are you going to do about that?' said Gerrity.

'I'm in the house by myself,' my father said. 'All I want is one room and I still have plenty of rooms left. You can leave the roof stripped if you want.'

Gerrity saw that he was determined not to pay any more money and went back to the men and told them. They all agreed to get on with the job and did an outstanding job on the roof. To this day, people still speak about the magnificent slated roof at Norman's Grove.

When my father was fifty years old, he married Edith Mary Quirke. My mother's mother was a McGrath from a well-known family in Ennis. One of her ancestors from around 1500 was Milo McGrath. We still have some of the furniture that came from the McGrath home in Kilbarron, which my mother brought with her.

My mother was born in Moyaghy, County Kildare, where her people had a farm on the Moore O'Ferrell estate. Her father went to school in Castleknock College and later took out a degree in engineering in Trinity. After working in Ireland for a number of years, he decided to move to Canada with his wife and three children.

It was decided that my mother would be left behind with an aunt until they were settled down. However, this never materialised and my mother stayed on in Belgrave Square in Dublin and spent many years looking after an invalid aunt.

The Canadian Pacific Railway from Montreal to Vancouver was being built at the time that my maternal grandfather went to Montreal. He worked on the Canadian Pacific Railway as an engineer for many years.

His son, my Uncle Eugene, went into the Ministry of Labour in Canada. He specialised in settling strikes. He was a very good-looking man with an excellent manner and was very good at his job. There were often strikes in the mining districts in the Arctic Circle and he was often up in that district for weeks at a time. He married a Miss Caroline O'Meara – one of the Limerick O'Mearas – and had two daughters, Patricia and Hortence. He had no sons, so the Quirke line is extinct.

My Aunt Rose was a nun and spent most of her life educating the Eskimos. She was very small, around the same size as an Eskimo, so they took to her very much. During the winter she came down to Calgary, because the weather was too severe for her in the Arctic Circle.

My Aunt Dillie was a French teacher in Brooklyn. She was a teacher of a very high standard, because she was awarded the Legion of Honour by the French government for her promotion of the French language in America. The reason that she was so good at French is that they were educated bilingually in English and French and then she went to McGill University to take out her degree. She visited Gunnocks about every second or third year and she was the only sister who came back here.

My Aunt Aileen died at the age of fifteen.

The other sister was Lilla, who was the nurse in the Gillette razor factory. As you can well imagine, she had a fair amount to do. I think she was practically all her life in Gillette and was then pensioned off. She lived in Montreal with her brother Eugene and her sister-in-law Carol.

There are a couple of reasons why my father did not marry until he was around fifty-five years of age. My mother knew my father for a number of years, but decided that she would not marry him until her aunt died, although I believe my father offered to have the aunt come along with her to Gunnocks. My father also wished to get his brothers settled and help them to buy land before he got married himself.

My mother never got to Canada, except on a visit in 1925, when she met her brother, and the two sisters who she had never met before. Her parents were both dead by this point.

I was born in 1909 when my father was fifty-nine years old and was my parents' only child. My mother died in 1928 and is buried in Loughsallagh cemetery beside my father, who died in 1938.

6

LOCAL CHARACTERS

THEIR METHODS AND THEIR MADNESS

When I was a boy, the local plumber was a man called Tommy Morrissey. My father used to call him Tom Morris and I have reason to believe that was his correct name. He lived near Gunnocks with his aunt Mrs Critchley, where Mrs Brennan lives now.

When Tommy left school, he was employed by the Thompson family as a herd, to look after the lands of Mayne. This is the same land that had previously been in corn and they were the people whose corn was eaten by rats. My father and my Uncle Michael used to rent Mayne to feed strippers and the Thompsons provided Tommy as a herd, or as a 'man'. Nevertheless, my father used to look through the cattle pretty constantly, because Tommy wouldn't be any great judge.

Tommy was a very colourful character and a very learned man, who learned most of what he knew from reading. Father used to call over to Mrs Critchley's house on a Sunday, to have a chat with Tom and to ask him about the cattle. On one particular day, he found to his surprise that he had not returned from counting the cattle, even though it was quite late. When he arrived back, father asked him whether he had had trouble finding the cows.

'Oh, the cows,' said Tom. 'I walked through every field in the place and I never thought of looking at the cows. Do you know what I was thinking about? I was thinking how I would make Walter Scott's *The Lady of the Lake* in fretwork.'

On another occasion when my father went to see Tom, he walked out of Mrs Critchley's house with a new repeating rifle. He told my father that this was the latest thing in guns and then he fired two shots into the air. Both men had their backs turned to the door of the house and did not see Mrs Critchley coming out of the house with a sweeping brush. She hit Tommy over the head with the first blow, driving his hat down hard on his head. The second blow got him across his shoulders.

'You ruffian,' she said. 'And my turkeys about to hatch!'

For anybody that doesn't know, a bad fright like that would kill young turkeys in the eggs. She was upset that, after three weeks of the hen sitting on the eggs, they might all die on account of him firing just one shot.

As Tommy got older, he became a plumber and there was plenty for him to do, because there was no other plumber in this part of the country. He got a lot of work in those big houses up in Clonsilla and he also worked here at Gunnocks. Tommy loved any amount of splashing the water around and leaking pipes and there would be lots of cleaning up afterwards, but he was very good at the job.

He was a heavy build of a man, very strong, and he always wore a hard hat. He had a big strong bicycle, which was reinforced by a second bar across the centre of the frame. That allowed him to carry quite a lot of piping, tools, blowlamps and all of the equipment he needed for soldering.

In many of the big houses where he worked, the fittings would have been very old. It was hard to get the exact type of fitting needed for a pipe, or a basin, or a toilet. Tommy used to cycle to Dublin every now and then and he used to visit the scrap yards.

There were two or three of them in the city at that time and the scrap metal would be built up in heaps of up to twenty feet. He would walk along and find various things such as bolts, nuts, flues, rods, taps, stoppers or even pieces of piping that he wouldn't be able to get in a shop. He'd spend a lot of time walking along the top of these heaps, which allowed him to spot the kind of thing that might be of use to him.

When he had collected them he went to the office and paid for the parts. It would be a small amount, because they would be glad to sell them. They had a whole shipload of scrap iron which would be sent to England to be melted down for various things.

He rode everywhere on his bike; he was a great man to ride. He wasn't a great churchgoer, so on a Sunday he's start off at daylight and he'd ride up to Blessington in Wicklow, which was twenty miles from where he lived and most of it was uphill. He'd tour all of that part of the country and then he'd come back in the evening time.

Tommy had a row with Father Bernard Brady, who was the parish priest of Dunboyne at the time. It was really amusing to me, as a boy. He'd be putting up a pipe or something of that kind in the house and as he was driving in the nails, each time he'd hammer he'd say, 'Ho, ho, Brady, there's one for you now! I hope that'll go into ya.'

Of if he had soldered a burst pipe he'd say, 'Oh ho, Brady, that'll stop ya now.'

He got on quite well with my uncle, Father John Ward. He'd say, 'Oh ho, you're a gentleman; you're not like Brady beyond.'

It's quite likely that Tommy was a Parnellite or had leanings that way, and the clergy were opposed to Parnell.

Over the course of the nineteenth century, political power in Ireland shifted from the Protestant Ascendency to the new Catholic middle classes. The main reasons for this were the abolition of the Penal Laws, the widening of the electoral franchise to all males regardless of their rank, property or education, throughout the United Kingdom over the course of the nineteenth century, and the organisation of the Irish Parliamentary Party by Charles Stuart Parnell.

Parnell was born in County Wicklow in 1846. He was the seventh child of John Henry Parnell, a wealthy Protestant landowner, and his American wife, Delia Stewart, the daughter of a naval hero of the American war of 1812 against the British, Commodore Charles Stewart.

He studied at Magdalene College, Cambridge, and entered parliament in 1875 as a member for County Meath, supporting the Home Rule party. In 1880, he was elected chairman of the Home Rule party and restructured it from top to bottom, creating a well-organised grass-roots structure and membership to replace the party's previous informal grouping.

Between 1879 and 1882, Parnell was involved with the Land League, which campaigned for the rights of tenant farmers in Ireland. In 1882, he changed the party's name to the Irish Parliamentary Party (IPP) and began to focus on the goal of legislative independence for Ireland, or Home Rule. Under his leadership, the party moved away from its liberal Protestant landlord tradition, and its new leaders were generally drawn from the Catholic middle class.

In the mid-1880s, the Conservative and Liberal parties were evenly matched and depended on the votes of the IPP to form a government. In the mid-1880s, Liberal Party leader William Gladstone committed his party to support the cause of Irish Home Rule, introducing the First Home Rule Bill in 1886. However, the measure failed to pass the British House of Commons, following a split between pro- and anti-Home Rulers within the Liberal Party.

In 1890, Parnell was named in the divorce papers of Captain Willie O'Shea and his wife, Katherine O'Shea. The ensuing scandal illustrates the hypocrisy of the times. It had been widely known among politicians at Westminster that Parnell was the long-term partner and father of three of the children of Katharine O'Shea. Captain O'Shea decided to initiate divorce proceedings after failing to secure a large inheritance that he had expected to receive from his wife's family.

The scandal split the IIP into Parnellite and anti-Parnellite factions. The Catholic Church spoke out against Parnell and the split in the IIP lasted more than a decade. Parnell married Katherine in 1891 and died a few months later.

Gladstone introduced the Second Irish Home Rule Bill in 1893. It passed the House of Commons, but was killed by the Conservative-dominated House of Lords.

The IPP re-formed in the early years of the twentieth century and a Home Rule bill was passed in 1914. The legislation was shelved for the duration of the First World War. However, by the end of the war, the Irish electorate had endorsed a more radical form of separatism and an armed struggle for independence had begun.

Parnell is best remembered for his involvement in the land-reform movement and for his achievement in convincing a British prime minister to introduce Home Rule legislation. The way in which he created a disciplined and highly organised political party became the model for all political parties in Britain and Ireland.

Tommy also had a black retriever dog, and he used to bring him along to jobs. The dog was a darn nuisance in the house, because Tommy would be working in the bathroom upstairs and he'd suddenly remember that he'd left his hat in the kitchen. He'd say to the dog, 'Go fetch my hat', and the dog would go down the stairs in leaps and bounds, so that if anybody was coming up there was the danger that he would have knocked them down.

At that time we had Mary Matthews as the housekeeper and she was lame, so there was always the danger that the dog would knock her down, but he never did. The dog would retrieve his hat, but he'd also retrieve a ham or something like that; Tommy had him well trained to go for it.

Then Tommy would start talking to himself upstairs, abusing Father Brady. Mary would think that he was calling for her, to turn off the water or you wouldn't know what he'd want. She'd say, 'What is it, Tommy?' because she wouldn't want to walk up the stairs. There would be no sound from Tommy because he'd suddenly realised that he was talking to himself and that the things he was saying weren't meant for anybody but himself.

He also carried out experiments, one of which was really dangerous. At one point he was living with his niece. He got the kettle, filled it with water and soldered the lid and the spout shut. That was so that no steam could come out of it when he put it on an open fire. When it reached boiling point, it exploded.

He hadn't told his niece about the experiment, but luckily she wasn't in at the time. It did a certain amount of damage around the house and a lot of people thought it was just going too far to have done such a thing. But he was that type of a man and that was that.

Another man called Curtis used to live at Norman's Grove, where he worked for my father. As part of his wages, Curtis was given three or four drills of potatoes; perquisites of that kind were normal in those days. He was anxious that they would all come up and he tended them carefully himself.

Norman's Grove had huge numbers of crows and he hated to see the crows coming near them. They settled in the trees every evening, perhaps fifty or one hundred of them, one lot after another. They'd be coming from the corn fields, where they'd gathered any amount of wheat that had shed on the ground.

'Look at those villains now,' Curtis said to my father. 'They're looking for praties to cool their bellies after all of that hot corn.'

Horace Plunkett, the founder of the agricultural co-operative movement, was born in England in 1854, the sixth child of Baron Dunsany. When he was six years old, his family moved to Dunsany, in County Meath. His family were Anglo-Norman landlords and were related to Saint Oliver Plunkett, a seventeenth-century Meath Catholic bishop who had been martyred by the English in Tyburn. Plunkett was from the

Protestant branch of the family, but they were on very friendly terms with his Catholic cousins, the Earls of Fingal, who lived in nearby Killeen Castle.

He was educated at Eton and Oxford and spent a number of years ranching in Wyoming. When he returned to Ireland, he started a co-operative store in Cork and a co-operative creamery in Limerick. In 1894, he started the Irish Agricultural Organisation Society (IAOS), which became a huge success. Four years later, there were 243 affiliated societies. By 1904, there were eight hundred societies in existence, with a trade turnover of £3 million. This included dairy societies, co-operative banks and agricultural societies, which had a combined membership of ninety thousand.

Plunkett persuaded farmers to form co-operatives to process and market their own butter, milk and cheese to standards suitable for the British market, rather than producing unhygienic, poor-quality food in their homes for local traders. This enabled farmers to deal directly with companies that they themselves owned, rather than allowing middlemen to absorb the profits.

He was appointed as a member of the Congested Districts Board, which sought to alleviate poverty in the west of Ireland by encouraging the local economy, consolidating uneconomic farms and resettling people in more prosperous regions.

Plunkett was elected as a unionist MP in the early 1890s. The Conservatives were in power at the time and had initiated a policy of 'killing Home Rule with kindness'. They introduced a number of initiatives in an attempt to persuade Irish people that the Union of Great Britain and Ireland was a better arrangement than Home Rule.

In 1898, the Conservative government set up the Department of Agriculture and Technical Instruction (DATI) to provide agricultural education, improvement and development to the Irish agricultural industry, and they put Plunkett in charge of this first-ever Irish ministry.

While the co-operative movement was the love of his life, politics was the bane of Plunkett's existence. He was dropped by the Irish Unionist Party for being too liberal, while his co-operative movement was opposed by nationalist politicians, who didn't believe that economic reform was any substitute for Home Rule.

During the War of Independence, co-operative creameries were attacked and burned by the British military, which saw them as centres of sedition. In 1921, the military closed the remaining creameries.

After the signing of the Anglo-Irish Treaty, Plunkett was nominated to the Irish Senate. However, his co-operative movement was split by partition. The Ulster Agricultural Organisation Society was founded in the new Northern Ireland state, while the IAOS was awarded an annual grant from the government of the Irish Free

State. During the subsequent Civil War, Plunkett's house was burned down by anti-Treaty IRA and he moved to England, where he died in 1932.

Many years ago, a young man by the name of Mr Black came to live at Courthill, in Dunboyne. He was the son of a wealthy Dublin merchant and his father was anxious that his son would live the life of a country gentleman: hunting, shooting and riding. Although he rented the house, garden and pleasure grounds at Courthill, I don't think that he rented the lands.

He did rent land near Strokestown, where he put sheep to graze. When it came to the end of June, the sheep had not been shorn and the wool was falling off them in lumps. One of the men from Gunnocks called on him, to ask whether he would like his sheep shorn. Black did not know what the man was talking about.

'You want to cut the wool off my sheep?' he said. 'Surely the sheep wants its wool the same way that you require your coat; you would not like me to take your coat.'

The herd told him that the wool would grow again.

'Well, if you want to cut the wool off my sheep, you can do so.'

'My charge for shearing the sheep is sixpence per head,' the herd told him.

'Oh, so now you want to charge me to cut the wool off my sheep,' Black said to the herd. 'Are you mad or do you think that I am mad? If you are so anxious to cut the wool off my sheep, then you can do so and keep it for yourself. But I will not pay you to do it.'

The man shore the sheep the following day and made a handy profit from selling the wool.

A well-known horse dealer from Dublin used to drive his turnout to Dunboyne on Sundays. A 'turnout' was a very good horse – both fast and well-mannered – and an excellent trap and harness. The dealer would take a drink in James Logan's and then drive his horse and car through the town and around the roads surrounding the village, to advertise his business. The turnout that he drove around Dunboyne would have been very expensive, but he had horses and traps of all kinds that would have cost less. He told one of the men working in Courthill that he would give him something for himself, if he would mention to Mister Black that a man in his position should have a really good horse and trap.

When Black heard about the horse dealer, he met with him and asked him to sell the turnout. The dealer said that he could not sell it, because it was the way in which he advertised his business. Not only that, but the horse was considered to be one of the fastest and best-mannered horses in Ireland.

Black was very interested in this and told the dealer that he would give him a very good price. The dealer said that he would not sell, but invited Black to come for a drive with him. They drove as far as the railway station and back again. After the drive, Black insisted on buying the turnout. The dealer agreed to sell, but at a very high price. Black gave him three times as much as the turnout was worth. However, both parties were satisfied with the transaction.

Mister Nedley lived on Nedley's Lane, which was more correctly known as Green Lane. My father said that Nedley was a very interesting man and they often travelled in the same carriage from Dunboyne to Broadstone Station in Dublin.

Nedley had travelled all over the world, working his way from place to place. He had spent many years diving for sponges off the coast of South America. While diving, he held his breath as long as he could before he resurfaced with the sponges, which grow at great depths. He rubbed oil on his body to get him down quickly and did not even wear a loin cloth in case it might hamper him.

After he Nedley retired, he moved to Harlockstown. He was a great walker. When he required something small for the house, that he was unable to get in Dunboyne, he walked into Dublin for it. He left early, so that he would be in Dublin by the time that the shop opened. He would buy his small parcel and walk home at once. It is eight Irish miles – ten English miles – from Gunnocks to O'Connell Street in Dublin's city centre.

On some days, he started out for the ten o'clock train from Dunboyne, but if he found that he had a half-hour wait, he would walk to Dublin rather than wait for the train.

Nedley had a large two-storey house. When he was leaving home for the day, he left all of the doors and windows open, because that would give the impression that he was about the place and people would not go inside. In those days, Green Lane was a great camping place for tinkers.

The Seagraves, who farmed at Vesington, which adjoined Nedleys, were smugglers. They brought small loads of hay and straw from Dunboyne to Portrane, which is in County Dublin by the Irish Sea. They collected wine, spirits, tobacco and cigars, placed the hay on top of them and brought the load back to Vesington. They used the same system to bring the goods to Dublin, where they were sold.

The excise men did not bother about them, because they thought that they were farmers on their way to sell farm produce. They had a large tunnel out in the land at Vesington, where they kept the contraband until it was time to sell it.

These Seagraves were the forebearers of the late Sir Henry Seagrave, the world-famous racing motorist and speedboat ace, who held the world speed record before the Second World War. He was killed while performing a speedboat test on Lake Como in Italy when his speedboat struck a small floating object.

In my father's time, 'tramps' were to be seen and met with in every part of the country. When I was a boy, we had a visit from a tramp almost every day and on some days we had four callers. The record was eleven in one day. All of the Ward families gave them food or clothes, but never money, because it was thought that they would spend it on drink.

Some of the tramps were on the road year-round. Others only took to the roads during the fine weather, between May and October. They spent the rest of the year with relatives, or in the county homes.

Some of them came on a regular day each week. The 'Wednesday Man' used to call every Wednesday, as he made his way to the Dublin cattle market to act as a drover on Thursday.

The man with the dead arm came at Christmas, dressed in riding clothes. He had hurt his arm in Milady's, a well-known horse dealer's stables in Islandbridge. Then there was 'Sleepy Paddy', who would lie in the sun as long as it shone and then he'd move off and just amble along the road.

Another tramp – although I don't know if he'd like to be called that or not – was Jack Stirabout, so called because he was always on the move. It was also a play on the word 'stirabout', which means porridge. He used to attend all of the fairs and would help to load cattle onto wagons. We used to give him a few shillings, but if you didn't, he would be very abusive. For the sake of peace, it was better to hand him something and he'd be quite satisfied with it.

Johnny and his mother, or 'Jack and his Ma', did not knock on the door, but sang songs such as 'Molly Brannigan' from some distance. They were a very gentle pair – the light of heaven to them.

Tom Steele was a north-of-Ireland Protestant, who had been a butler in a big house until he went a bit simple. Most of the tramps were affected in this way. Steele used to call to the hall door at Norman's Grove at dinner time and ask to see Christopher Ward in person. This was unusual. In general, all tramps called to the back door, which was the kitchen door.

When grandfather came to the door, Steele would say, 'The roast beef smells very good today, I will have some now.'

Steele had a sarcastic turn of phrase. He called to the yard at Nuttstown looking for help and Joe Meehan ordered him away. He then went to Norman's Grove, asked to see grandfather and told him that 'the cow's butler' had ordered him away.

All of the tramps had great praise for the Fieldstown Wards, where they were given tea, even during the war years, when it cost thirty shillings per pound on the black market. My uncle used to collect it every Thursday from a Belfast cattle dealer named McGovern during the Second World War.

On one occasion, Miss Kehoe, the housekeeper in Fieldstown, went to New Barn House, an old wreck of a place where the tramps stayed when they were near Fieldstown. A strange tramp was present and was most abusive towards her. My uncle went to New Barn that evening and gave out to all the tramps there about their member. The next day a deputation came to apologise to Miss Kehoe and brought the erring member with them.

My father also told me about a man who was always looking for a 'mag's nest'. He meant a magpie's nest. He'd climb up high trees looking for the nests, but he wasn't in his right mind. Once some men, a nasty few, saw him up in the tree. They had a saw and pretended to be cutting down the tree. The unfortunate man thought that the tree had fallen and jumped out of it. He wasn't hurt, but it wasn't a nice thing to do.

Another character, Dan Cunningham, was a tailor by profession. In those days, tailors went to the customer's house and measured them. The customer bought the material required to make a jacket, waistcoat and trousers. When the material had been bought, Dan would come to the customer's house and make the clothes. When the customer came in for his dinner, they would try on the clothes to see how they fit, and when he came in for his tea he would try on some other part of the clothes.

Dan lived in a house with a small plot of ground, every corner of which was cultivated with onions, cabbage and salad. When he'd have a small amount he would bring it into the Dublin market on his horse and cart, which had a plank nailed across it on which he sat. He only had a small amount of produce and would make two shillings, or two shillings and sixpence.

Dan was afraid of robbers. When he was travelling home in the winter he used to talk to himself in different voices, arguing with himself, to convince would-be robbers that there were a number of people in the cart.

Both he and his wife were extremely tall and they had no family. The day his wife died, Dan locked the door of the house and went into the market with his onions and cabbage. Somebody stopped him in Clonee and told him that he shouldn't go to the market that day, because his wife was dead in the house and it wasn't the thing to do.

'Well', he said, 'I must go, because we can't live be the dead.'

7

FATHER BERNARD BRADY AND FATHER GRENNAN

The Wards were a strong Catholic family, but they were not the kind of Catholics who let the priest rule them. In my father's time and in my daughter Olivia's time, they would not stand for any browbeating by the priest of the parish.

In the diocese of Meath, there is a horrible practice known as 'the table'. During a funeral, while the coffin was still up at the altar, the parish priest brought out a table. He covered it and left it at the head of the coffin.

The idea was that each person in the church went up and put a donation on the table, which was for the benefit of the priest. The nearest relatives were expected to give the most money and the amounts tapered off down to the people who didn't know the family well, but who might have done business with them. Those people would throw sixpence or a shilling onto the table.

It was a rather reprehensible practice in my opinion and in the opinion of a great many others. My grand-uncle, John Ward, was determined to put a stop to the practice. During the funeral of one of his sisters, the priest came out, set up the table and put the white cloth over it. John walked up to the table and stood with his back to it, looking out to the people.

'It is high time that we in this parish put a stop to holding an auction over the dead,' he said. 'Let nobody come up here with any money.'

He stood there to ensure that nobody came up. From that day to this, there has never been a collection at the head of the coffin in Dunboyne. However, the custom has continued in every other church in the diocese, except perhaps Navan and Kells.

My father often spoke of Father Bernard Brady, who was the parish priest of Dunboyne back around 1870. He came from the part of Meath that borders Offaly, on the way down to Tullamore.

Father Brady was a very learned man, but he was not very popular with the people; he put himself on a higher stage than the average person and was very literary. Undoubtedly, he gave marvellous sermons, some of which were very cutting.

At that time, the parish priest in Dunboyne owned a farm. It was a comparatively small farm, located where GAA coach Sean Boylan now lives, at the foot of the railway bridge in Dunboyne. The Boylans got divided land from the Irish Land Commission in the 1930s and extended their farm.

The Wards were very strong Catholics and a man from Gunnocks ploughed, sowed and reaped on the parochial farm. The priest also used to have his Sunday dinner in Gunnocks and brought the collections from both masses to Gunnocks with him each week.

The herds from the Gunnocks – Jim and George Earley – looked after the cattle for him. George Earley had a wonderful sense of humour; he was full of fun, jokes and tricks and kept the people in the district laughing at all the things he said and did.

George hated the hunting people. He didn't hate the country hunting man, but a lot of city people used to come out to this area to hunt. They were professional people and the like, and they thought that they owned the place. They were absolutely obnoxious. They were also unable to keep up with the hunt; really they were only out for exercise. When they lost the hunt, they'd stop and ask for directions. George had a way of talking to them, if they asked him for directions.

'There there, my man, there there,' they'd say. 'Which way did the hunt go?'

George would pretend to be some kind of uneducated kind of fool, which he wasn't by any means.

'Well, now,' he'd say. 'If they're gone on as they were goin' on, they're in Gallydary's lawn, begob.'

Then the man would whip up his horse and ride off without having got any information of value from him.

He also used to play tricks on his brother Jim. There used to be a plank bridging the ditch between the lawn and the house field. There was a well-beaten path across the lawn to the plank.

In an odd year, the grass grew quite long on both sides of the path and George would go out, make a few loops in the grass and tie the grass from one side to the other. Then he'd say to Jim, 'Come on quick, master wants the cattle up from the paling in a hurry.'

Jim would run quickly along the path, catch his foot, and down he'd go. Then he'd go on a few yards and would fall over again.

'What's wrong with you, what are you falling for?' George would say.

'Oh, I don't know what's wrong with me; I'm after catching my foot,' and then he'd go down a third time.

George kept Father Grennan well supplied with stories of happenings and scandals that were supposed to be taking place in the parish, but which never actually happened. Sometimes he carried it too far. From time to time he would say to Father Grennan, 'I suppose you heard about the scandal that happened at such-and-such a place in the parish?'

Father Grennan was an extremely holy man, but he was completely unworldly, even by the standards of that time.

He would tell George that he hadn't heard, and George would tell him all about it. Father Grennan would get upset and would load up the horse and cart to see the family or person concerned.

When he got there he would give the people a bit of his mind about the matter, without ever listening to what they had to say. They would plead their innocence but it would be of no avail. If George Early said it, it must be correct.

My father used to mention a man by the name of Tom Brown. The Browns had been in America and had returned home and bought a farm. They lived where Johnny Curry lives now and had bought the farm where Larry Goodman has his corn store, near Ballymagillan Stud. Tom Brown didn't practise any kind of religion whatsoever, but he had a saying, that my father thought was very true. 'Religion,' he'd say. 'It's the best policeman.'

In those days people rarely went to confession or Holy Communion. Some people only went during the Easter period, but most people went twice a year. Father Grennan used to hear confession before mass in the sacristy – or the vestry, as it was called – and only one or two people would go on any particular occasion.

He never bothered to shut the door of the vestry. In most cases it didn't make any difference. However, there was one particular man who was very rough. If there was any kind of an argument, he would draw back and hit the other man in the jaw. He was on various committees and had a good deal of standing in the parish.

He lived about two miles from the town of Dunboyne and always carried a blunderbuss – a gun – with him wherever he was going. I asked my father whether there was any reason he should carry it, wondering whether he was unpopular or if he had taken possession of disputed land. However, my father told me that it was supposed to lend him prestige.

He used to go to confession every now and then and carried the blunderbuss into the chapel with him. There were wooden altar rails and a wooden kneeling board at the top of the chapel. When he reached the gate of the altar rails, on his way into the vestry, he threw the unloaded blunderbuss against the railing. From the time he walked into the vestry, you could see the blunderbuss slipping slowly along the altar rails until it fell.

Possibly one of the reasons why it moved so much was that when this man went into confession, he shouted at Father Grennan at the top of his voice. That was completely unnecessary, but he was that kind of a man. Most people in the chapel heard what he was saying to Father Grennan. It was embarrassing, but this man didn't seem to mind.

After a while the blunderbuss would slip far enough that it would fall to the ground and make a loud noise on the tiled floor. The people watching would be very glad when it fell, because it took away the tension in the chapel.

Sometimes, when he was in confession, another man would enter the chapel and kneel in the place where he had been kneeling before he went into confession. He didn't take kindly to that, so he caught the man by the collar, pitched him out in the passage and took his place.

Father Grennan used to take the collection after the Gospel reading. As was usual at that time, he would go from seat to seat collecting the money. What was unusual about Father Grennan's method was that, as he worked his way down the chapel, he would see somebody with whom he wished to chat; perhaps about the running of the parish.

In those cases, Father Grennan told the person sitting beside the man with whom he wished to speak, to get out into the passage so that they could have a conversation. Sometimes the issue couldn't be resolved without a third person, so another person would be displaced from the pew so that Father Grennan and both of his men could have a long conversation.

The most annoying thing was when one of the parishoners would want to speak to him on a private matter, perhaps a matrimonial matter. As soon as Father Grennan understood the nature of the matter, he cleared the people out of that seat, the seat in front of it and the seat behind.

This chat could go on for some time before people were called back to their seats and he would continue with the collection.

People also asked him questions as he walked down the chapel. The man with the blunderbuss would call out to him, 'Would Mary Bolton have a clutch of duck eggs?' Mary Bolton was Father Grennan's housekeeper and she kept hens and ducks.

'Ha-ha,' he'd say. 'I'll ask her when I go home; I'll ask her when I go home.'

On another occasion, Father Grennan put the collection box in front of a man with a particularly big moustache and said, 'I think you have the ugliest moustache in the parish.'

The whole ceremony took a very long time. Most people would have had their breakfast before they came to mass, unless they were taking communion. They didn't have anywhere to go afterwards, unless there was a spell of fine weather after a very bad spell of weather, in which case they might have to make hay. Otherwise, they wouldn't think of working on a Sunday, it just wasn't the done thing.

One Sunday, Father Grennan was riding his horse over to Kilbride to say mass. His curate couldn't afford a horse, so he took shortcuts across the fields, but Father Grennan rode around the roads.

At that time, there was a bedridden old woman living on voluntary land by the side of the road to Kilbride. Father Grennan used to visit her every Sunday and have a conversation with the poor woman. This went on for years, until Father Grennan arrived one day and she told him to kneel and say a few prayers for her.

'Let me go on out of this,' she said. 'I'm long enough lying down here in the bed.'

She didn't seem any different on that day to any other occasion, but he knelt beside the bed and covered his eyes to pray. When he had finished his prayers, he looked up and found – to his surprise – that she was dead. She had been waiting for him to come to say the prayers, so that she could be let go out of that, as she said herself.

The stations in our locality used to take place twice every year. Stations are a custom whereby the local priest celebrates mass in one of the local houses. I presume these are a continuation of when mass was celebrated in houses during the penal years. In other parts of the country there were public stations, which meant that the station rotated between a number of houses in the district over the course of three or four years.

This was a big undertaking for the wife of the household, because all of the local people came into the station in the house. Where there was a large population in the area, the numbers were quite big.

Each family knew the year and the month in which their station fell due. The yard and the outside of the house were whitewashed, or limewashed. The inside of the house was whitewashed too; not just the interior walls, but the furniture and the beds too.

Father Conlon – who succeeded Father Grennan as the parish priest in Dunboyne – told me that he attended public stations in Longford that had a very large attendance. In that situation, the local women came in to assist the woman of the house.

The mass took place first and then all of the men went outside for a smoke or a walk, while one group of women cut the bread and another group buttered it. They had big white covers over one of the double beds and as they buttered the bread they threw it onto the cover of the bed.

The priest was given his breakfast in a small living room. The ordinary people who came got their food in the kitchen; they collected a mug of tea, collected a slice or two of bread off the bed and went outside to eat it, because there wouldn't have been room for the whole lot of them in the house.

The late Master Donnegan, who was the schoolmaster in Dunboyne and who taught me as a boy – and taught me very well indeed, as well as any school I was ever sent to – told me the following story. He came from near Rosemount, which is a few miles from Moate, in County Westmeath.

He was an altar boy at one of the public stations, at which there were a large number of people. Everything that was needed for the mass was kept in a box. The box was an ingenious thing; the sides could be lowered until the entire box lay flat on the table. The box itself contained everything needed for the mass, including the vestments and the chalice. The prayers of the mass were written on both the floor and the back of the box. When the mass was over, it was reassembled using clips, the vestments were placed inside and it was brought back to the parochial house for the next station.

The box was brought to the station on an outside car. On this occasion, it turned out that they had forgotten to put the chalice into the box. When the parish priest discovered this, somebody was sent to get it.

The men of the family asked their sister where the priest had gone.

'Ah, he's in the sitting room saying his prayers.'

'Look it, get the breakfast ready for him and give it to him now before he starts to say mass; that will quicken things up a bit.'

Of course, any Catholic would know that he couldn't say mass after having his breakfast.

When Father Brady heard this story from Master Donnegan, he drily remarked, 'Well, I think he would have been much better out in the kitchen, trying to educate the ignorant, than to be in the sitting room saying his prayers.'

In this part of the country there were what I call 'private stations'. The private station consisted of the two priests coming over, saying two masses in the house, having their breakfast, having a discussion after breakfast, and then leaving to carry out their parochial work. Anybody who wished to take communion or go to confession could do so as well. Both of the priests got a donation for saying mass in the house.

Master Donnegan also told me about the very gentlemanly approach that Father Brady had towards people. There was a certain woman who lived near the church who could often be very difficult about certain matters with regards to the church grounds. Mr Donnegan came back with a report to Father Brady from her and Father Brady's remark was, 'She is the stubborn reed'.

Father Conlon – who was the parish priest after Father Grennan – was much more outspoken. Father Conlon had difficulty with this same woman in regards to church property and he said to Mr Donnegan, 'I was down with that old woman and there's a terrible lot of the sow about her.'

Because the Ward family were prominent parishoners, they knelt in the front pew of the church gallery in Dunboyne.

When my father was a small boy, there were geese on the green in Dunboyne, which belonged to somebody in the town. My father was afraid of the geese, because they'd give you a nasty bite if you went too near them. The curate knew this, so he used to frighten him by running after him and calling him a goose.

On one occasion, he was kneeling in the front gallery with his parents. When he saw the curate coming out to say mass he shouted out, 'Ha-ha, the geese can't get me up here'.

Of course, his parents told him that he shouldn't have said that, but he had got his revenge on the priest anyway.

I'll tell a little story about Bishop Fogarty of Killaloe. He lived in Ennis and was very nationalistic, much more than any of the other bishops at the time. I believe that he was one of the treasurers of the Sinn Féin funds.

He was a learned and cheerful man and he told the story about travelling up to Dublin by train. When he got to Newbridge – the station for the Curragh camp, which was a large British garrison at that time – a soldier who had too much drink taken fell into the carriage and sat down in front of him.

The soldier looked at him for some time and said, 'You're a priest.'

'Yes,' said Bishop Fogarty. 'Yes.'

'You're a parish priest?'

'I was yes,' he said. 'I was a parish priest'.

'Uh-huh,' said the soldier. 'You're a curate.'

'I was a curate,' said Bishop Fogarty.

'Put it there, you're the same as myself,' said the soldier, holding out his hand to him. 'Going down in the ranks: a sergeant yesterday and a private today.

I remember the confession boxes in the old church, where the priest sat on one side of the box and the penitent sat on the other. There wasn't any roof on the boxes and they were situated under the stairs going up to the gallery.

On one occasion, when there was a mission on, there was seat after seat of people waiting to go to confession. A local chimney sweep, who was a small man, was kneeling on the stairs. He wanted to get into confession quickly, so when one person walked out of the box, he just vaulted over the railings, into the top of the confession box and onto the kneeling board, ahead of forty or fifty other people.

During another mission, there were a large number of people waiting to have their confessions heard and some people were trying to get in front of other people. In this particular case, there was a hubbub outside the confession box, with loud talking and pushing. The confessor pulled back the curtain and put his head out.

'What's going on out here,' he asked.

'Ah,' said a boy. 'They won't let me in and they're pushing me back and I'm here so long and it's not fair.'

'How long are you here?' the confessor asked.

'Oh, I'm here since the time the woman told you that she staul the turkey.'

I'll tell another story about two painters, by the names of Curry and Rice, who were great friends with one another. They worked together, taking contracts to paint four or five of the railway stations on the Great Northern Line, from Malahide to Balbriggan. They tendered for these jobs every couple of years.

They had a third friend, by the name of Weldon; I forget what business he was in, but he used to go around with Curry and Rice. They were all very witty, and father said that on one occasion when they were painting the station at Donabate, Weldon came down and shouted, 'Oh, good morning, Curry and Rice', and he took his hat off to them. Either Curry or Rice replied, 'Aye, but mind you, it's Weldon too.'

In those days, a lot of people travelled by train and there would be any number of people to hear the thing and enjoy the fun of it. On another occasion, Curry and Rice were painting the railway station and were calling over and back to Weldon.

'Indeed, this is the first Friday and I'll bet you never went to mass,' Weldon said.

'Sure,' they replied, 'if we didn't go to mass, aren't we doing the stations anyway?'

8

THE YARD AT GUNNOCKS

The yard at Gunnocks has changed very little over the last hundred years. All the buildings are the same ones that I remember as a boy. The little yard lies outside the kitchen door, surrounded by a wall and a coal house which stored coal and timber for the winter.

We used to go to the Timahoe bog in County Kildare every year for turf. Three men would leave Gunnocks at daylight on a Monday, taking six horses and carts. The turf was stacked along the side of the road and the men helped to load it. They received the turf as part of their wages, as we used coal. When coal could be drawn from the boats for between one pound to thirty shillings per ton, my father gave the men coal instead. He didn't like giving two pounds per ton for coal.

There used to be a pump outside the kitchen door, but it was moved to the wall outside the little yard, even though it continued to pump water from the same spring. I remember when the pump was used to pump water into a stone trough that could be used to wash things; usually to wash the clay off vegetables that had been dug up. There was a bung in the trough which could be removed to drain the water from the trough.

The spring water around here is extremely hard, because it is very high in lime. The lime accumulates in kettle and buckets and after a while they get very heavy and are no longer suitable for boiling or using. At some point, the Wards erected a large water tank to collect the soft water from the gutters of the house. A new pump was erected at the base of the tank, so when there was no rain, water could be pumped up to the water tank.

Ward as a young man

Christopher Ward with two of his sons

Joe Ward's grandfather Christopher

Mary Jane Ward, *c.* 1868

Father John Ward CM at the time
of his ordination in Paris, *c.* 1890

Laurence Ward of Gunnocks,
c. 1890

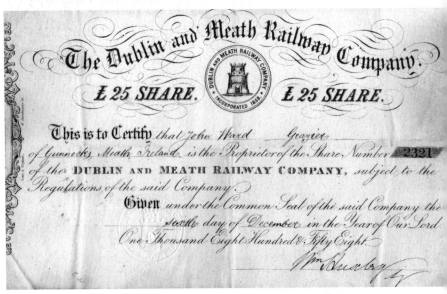

Dublin and Meath Railway Company share belonging to John Ward, 1858

rence Ward of Fieldstown East, *c.* 1890

John Ward's voter-registration card, 1836

Gun licence issued to Christopher Ward, 1848, during the period of the Young Ireland rebellion

unnocks in the 1970s. The farmhouse is in the foreground, with the coach house imme-
ately behind it. The old cow-house – which was originally a dwelling – is on the left.

unboyne Church and Parochial House

Received from Mr Laurence Ward
the Sum of One Hundred & Seven pounds twelve Shillings &
Sterj being for One Half Years Rent due me
out of a Holding in Loughsallagh & Roане
due and ending the First day of November
last Dublin Received this 22nd day of December
one thousand eight hundred & twenty four

£ 107. 12. 5   James Corballis

Rent receipt from Corballis landlords, 1824

Loyal National Repeal Association

GOD SAVE THE QUEEN   IRELAND FOR THE IR[...]

IRELAND

One Shilling is enrolled as a Repealer, in the Books of the
Association this 17 day of June 1844
Thos Matw Ray Secretary.

Repeal card, 1844

...ard family group, *c.* 1890. Back row, from left: Patrick and Ita Ward, Laurence Ward of ...unnocks, Mr Cannon, Michael Ward. Middle row: Laurence Ward of Fieldstown and ...ances Ward. Front row: Mary Ward, Maria Cuffe and Bridget Ward. Sarah Ward is kneel-...g at the front.

Fieldstown East, with
Laurence Ward of
Gunnocks in the foreground
and two of his sisters in the
background

Gunnocks in 1912. Laurence Ward is in the trap, and his wife Edith is standing beside
him. Mary Matthews, who worked in the house and looked after Joseph, is on the
right of the picture, and Jem Early is the man holding the horse's bridle.

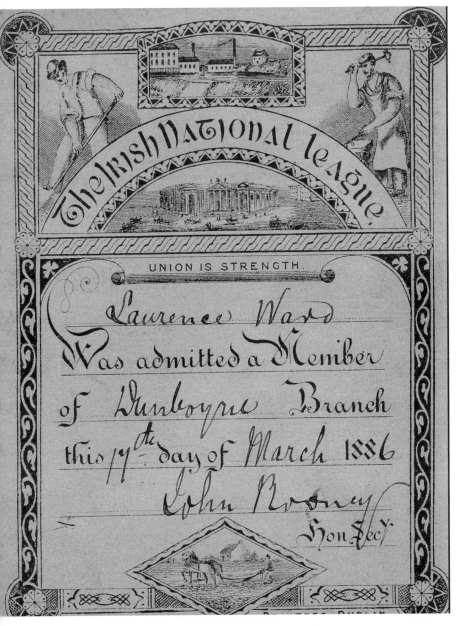

The Irish National League

UNION IS STRENGTH.

Laurence Ward

Was admitted a Member

of Dunboyne Branch

this 17th day of March 1886

John Rooney

Hon Secy

Laurence Ward's Land League membership card, 1886

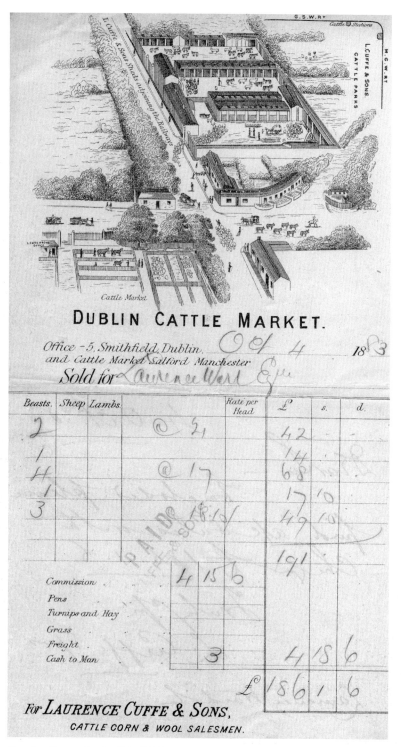

DUBLIN CATTLE MARKET.

Office – 5, Smithfield, Dublin,   Oct 4   18 83
and Cattle Market, Salford, Manchester

Sold for Laurence West Esq

Beasts.	Sheep	Lambs.			Rate per Head	£	s.	d.
2				@ 21		42		
1						14		
4				@ 17		68		
1						17	0	
3				18 10		49	10	
						191		
Commission			4	15	6			
Pens								
Turnips and Hay								
Grass								
Freight								
Cash to Man			3			4	18	6
					£	186	1	6

For LAURENCE CUFFE & SONS,
CATTLE CORN & WOOL SALESMEN.

Receipt for cattle, Cuffe's, 1882

air Day in Ballinamore, County Leitrim

(Reproduced courtesy of the National Photographic Archive)

air Day in Clonmel, County Tipperary

(Reproduced courtesy of the National Photographic Archive)

The Dublin cattle markets on the North Circular Road

(Reproduced courtesy of the National Photographic Archive)

R.I.C.

Dunboyne.

The bearer. Mr L. Ward
J.P. and his coachman
Mathew Ward are loyal
subjects of His Majesty,
and can be trusted to
enter the City.

James Malone
Constable

RIC permit for Laurence to travel to
Dublin during the 1916 Rising

Joe and Lilla Ward on their wedding day, 26 April 1938. Tom Condra is on the left, Phyllis Lloyd is next to Lilla, and Dan Doyle is on the right.

Clockwise from bottom left: Laurence, Michael, Patrick and Father John at Joe's wedding at the Hotel Russell on St Stephen's Green in Dublin, 1938. This photograph appeared on the front page of the *Irish Times* under the headline 'FOUR BROTHERS OVER EIGHTY'.

It was a troublesome job, because a man had to pump it from the well using a handle. A number of years ago, the idea of using small motors to pump the water was introduced and that did away with the pumping of the water into the tank.

The tank dates from 1905, when my mother came here to be married. At that point there was no bathroom or toilet in the house, which was typical for most of the big houses throughout the country. There was only the brick toilet in the woods, which was called 'the little house'. You can imagine what it was like in snowy weather, going out there. My mother put her foot down; she said that she had come from a city and was used to an indoor closet and insisted that a bathroom and toilet be erected at Gunnocks.

When you go through the gate from the little yard to the large yard, you come to a double-door building, which is the coach house. That building was used for the keeping of traps. We also had a brougham; it had four wheels and was pulled by just one horse. I remember that at one point it was pulled by a mare called Gary. It brought us to Dublin in about half an hour. When I say Dublin, I mean to the old Dublin cattle market in Phibsborough.

It was luxuriously upholstered with leather, which would have been padded with fibre. The brougham carried two people comfortably on the back seat. There were also two small seats on the front, which folded up and disappeared into the brougham.

The coachman sat outside on a high seat over the horses. There was a box or a cavity under his seat, where things could be stored. The coachman had a frieze coat, which went down to his ankles. It was very heavy and made from waterproof material which was extremely warm. He would also have worn gloves for holding the reins.

There was another trap that held four or five people. It was a high trap and was very well sprung. The shafts were made of a fibrous wood, which were very springy. If you went over a bump or a stone you didn't feel it very much. If the shafts broke, they didn't break cleanly.

There were two other small traps which were pulled by Iceland ponies. They were brought to Ireland from Iceland by dealers who brought them in large numbers and drove them in the same way you'd drive a drove of cattle. They were shown in the middle of Smithfield, or at the old Haymarket. The price might have been ten or twelve pounds, which would have been a good price, but it might have been a good deal less than that.

They were very strong, very docile and mostly old. They were usually a steel grey, with white or brownish colours, rather like the Connemara pony, but smaller. They were very easy to train, they were very sure-footed and rarely ever stumbled. They trotted all of the time and it was very hard to get them to walk. It was particularly hard when you were coming back from Dublin, because they knew they were going home.

The traps they drew, which were made in Ireland, were light and, even if there were five or six people in the trap,, it wasn't any heavier on the pony than if there was only one person in the trap because of the springs and because of the balance on the straddle. The least little tip of your centre finger on the shaft balanced the thing and you knew whether it was too heavy on them.

If my father was making an ordinary trip to Clonee or Dunboyne he'd take one of these traps, and if he was going to the land he'd take the other one. Sometimes he'd drive himself. If he was going for a canter he'd have one of the men with him, like Jim Earley.

The problem with bringing a trap into a field was that when you were opening a gate, the pony would want to eat the grass. If you didn't have your mind on it, they'd pull up in the middle of a field and start to eat the grass.

Just beyond the coach house was a cattle house that was known as the new house. I've no idea why it was called that, but presumably it was built after the other houses.

In those days cattle were always tied by the neck. They were never left loose in a shed because they all had horns and would do damage to each other if they weren't tied.

The house held a large number of cattle and there was a manger against the back wall. There's a channel that the manure and urine ran into. There were two doors on it through which the bedding and manure were thrown into the yard. Sometimes the men would be in a hurry and it might be left there for a day or two. When my father married my mother, she objected very strongly to seeing heaps of manure thrown outside the door. She clamped down and no more cattle were allowed in that house. It was turned into a house for keeping implements, palings, posts and small machines, such as the turnip pulper.

The turnip pulper was also used for crushing cattle cake, which was made from some kind of Indian corn and which was imported from the River Plate in South America, from Uruguay or Argentina.

It came in hard slabs, which were around two feet wide and three feet long. It was very rich in oil, was very fattening, and the animals loved it. The oil seeped through their skin and into their hair: if you rubbed your hand on their backs after a few weeks of feeding them cattle cake, your hand would be covered in brown oil.

You could buy it in hemp bags from agents, but it was much cheaper if you bought it straight from the boat. It was much cheaper than ordinary corn, or anything you could produce in this country.

There were certain farmers around here, feeding large numbers of cattle, who would buy five or six hundred tons of the stuff to throw up in the loft.

There is a loft over this cattle shed as well, but I don't ever remember anything in it except for hay.

Then there was a row of stables for keeping horses at the end of the yard. The Wards kept several horses and mares, as well as a number of one-, two- and three-year-old replacements. Some young horses were trained each year for farm work and were later sold in the Dunboyne, Drogheda and Swords horse fairs.

These horses were clipped once a year. In those days clippers had not been invented, or if they were, they weren't used around here. Instead, a comb and scissors were used in the same way an older man gets his hair cut nowadays.

A man called Andy Gogarty, from Mullanahob, Kilbride, came to clip the horses, and it was an event that everyone enjoyed. The horses that were to be clipped that night had been left in all day to dry off and had been very well brushed. The stable where the horses were to be clipped had plenty of clean dry straw on the floor. The men came home from the fields at dark, they had their tea, and then they came back to the yard. One man held the horse and the other men took turns holding the candles to give light.

When Andy was cutting the hair off the horse's underbelly, he lay on his back and the hair and dust fell into his mouth and his eyes. People who deal with horses will appreciate the risk he took when working a scissors between the horse's hind legs, while lying on his back under the animal. I never heard my father say that the horse stood on him.

Tea and home-made cakes were served to everybody during the night. Work finished at eleven o'clock and Andy walked home, to come back the next night. The men and Andy told stories all night. My father and his brothers were boys at the time, but he never told me any of the stories.

Beyond the stables, there was a second coach house. There was another loft over the second coach house, which was used for storing corn and oats. Sometimes the grain wasn't dry enough when it was brought in, so on rainy days two men would turn it backwards and forwards. They used to fill the loft to a depth of two feet and leave two yards free at the end, so that they would have room to turn it. Once it was perfectly dry it was ground up, mixed with cattle cake and fed to the cattle.

The big cattle yard was beside the second coach house. The manure and bedding from the cattle was built into a big heap in the centre of that; the pile might be six feet tall and twenty yards by thirty yards. It was left there to season and become properly rotten before it was put onto the potato drills. So some of the heap was left there for more than a year and every year the older part was used.

Beyond that you had the house that we called the lodge, which was where the yard man slept. In County Meath he'd be referred to as a man who was 'on the table'; this meant that he was fed three meals a day in the house, at the kitchen table.

On the wall of the lodge, you can see the mirror where he would shave himself, and there was a stove which burned wood or coal. You didn't need a very big stove, because of the size of the place.

When he got married, he got a house of his own and would move out. When Mattie Ward gave up being the yardman, the place was turned into a harness room, to keep the harnesses of the ponies and horses that pulled the brougham and the traps.

The old cow house was beyond the lodge. The house is pretty much the same way now as it was when it was built a few hundred years ago. I have no doubt that it was originally a dwelling house, probably for a herd. It is typical of the houses of the time, built from 'yalla clay and bullock's blood'.

The larger portion of the house was a very large kitchen. It had a huge open fireplace in the middle of the house, with a chain hanging down the chimney, from which they hung a pot for boiling. There were also two hobs in the fireplace for boiling other things. They left a pot of tea on the hob all day. They'd add a drop of water to it every now and then, until they had plenty of good strong black tea any time they wanted it.

The children slept in beds at the end of the room, where it would always be nice and warm. The smaller section of the house, behind the fireplace, was the room where the husband and wife slept.

Across the yard from the old cow house is the horse stable, where the working horses, Irish draught horses, were kept, which was seperate to the stables for the mares and foals. The stable had two loose stalls and one centre stall where the horse was tied.

There was a loft over the horse stable with three apertures or holes in the floor, for letting hay down to the horses. The holes were above the manger, so all you had to do was to shove the loose hay down to the horse. If there was a change of hay, the horses would refuse to eat it for the first couple of days. This would be true even when the second lot of hay was much better that the first. They knew the difference in the flavour. They'd be whinnying out through the window until they got hungry. Then they'd eat it.

The horse stable had racks which held the harnesses, the collars, and other sections of the harnesses. On a wet day the ploughman put dubbin and oil onto the harnesses' leather to keep it pliable and soft, and they shone the brass on the harnesses.

The lining of the harnesses was stuffed with horse hair and every now and then the wear and tear would make a hole in the lining. When it got worn it had to be brought to a straddler: a man who mended harnesses. The local menders were Goodwins in Mulhuddart, County Dublin, who are still there today.

My cousin Johnny Gallon, who had a linen factory in Balbriggan, County Dublin, told me that the patterns of the linings were specific to each county. People in Kerry might expect two blue lines and one white. People in Cork might expect two lines down and one across. In Meath and Dublin it might be four lines down and two across. Johnny told me that if he brought the wrong pattern from the factory in Balbriggan to a harness maker in Kerry, he'd refuse to accept it. It seems strange that they bothered about a detail that nobody could actually see.

You had to be extremely careful that the collar fitted perfectly. If it frayed the horse's neck in any way and if he got a pimple – the expression was a 'warble' – then he wouldn't work. He'd be like a person with a boil on their neck, he wouldn't be able to turn his head.

There is an interesting story relating to harnesses and Norman's Grove, which is worth recording. My father's mother was living there at the time.

Around 1870, there were two nuns who used to travel the length and breadth of Ireland, collecting for their convent, visiting each district every few years. They started collecting around May and finished sometime in October, and it was assumed that they returned to their convent sometime in October, for the winter months.

They became known as 'the two nuns', and they travelled in a brougham driven by a coachman. The procedure was that they went into a certain district, where they selected a house – a good house, one of the big houses – where they were put up for one or two nights, while they collected around the area for their convent.

When they came to collect around Dunboyne they always stayed a night with my grandmother in Norman's Grove and she used to make a little bit of extra fuss for the good nuns when they came to stay in the house.

At the time I'm talking about, nuns were very strict and did not eat their food with other people, but ate among themselves. When the two nuns arrived at a house, usually in the evening, they had their meal by themselves and went up to their bedroom, so there was very little conversation with them. They went out early to collect after their breakfast and didn't come back again until evening, so very little was known about them.

Before going to their room in the evening, they always impressed on the owner of the house that, when they were being called in the morning, a jug of hot water was to be handed into the room at the same time. Everyone noticed that and said, 'Wouldn't you think that the nuns would do it with cold water the same as everybody else,' but they insisted on it and they got it.

The nuns' coachman was also put up either in the house or the yard. James Rodgers, the yardman in Norman's Grove, did not like their coachman. He made it very clear to my grandmother that he didn't think the man was altogether straight, but she wouldn't hear of such a terrible thing. She said that he was a decent man and all the rest of it.

James Rodgers came to Norman's Grove from Saucerstown, near Swords, as a young man in the early 1850s. He was a brother-in-law of Curtis, mentioned earlier in Chapter 6, who hated crows. He lived to be a very old man, dying sometime around 1919. His youngest daughter was Mrs Nannie Hogarty, who died only a few years ago, in the 1960s.

On one occasion, the nuns' coachman told him that the horse's collar was fraying at its neck. The following morning, when they were leaving, Rodgers went into the harness room and found one of the harnesses missing and the nuns' harness hanging there instead.

The nuns had to drive down the avenue to leave Norman's Grove and Rodgers was able to run across the front lawn and intercept them before they got out onto the main Dublin-to-Navan road. They pulled up and he pointed out to the man that, by mistake, he must have taken the wrong horse collar.

The nuns, according to Rodgers, were very upset indeed and reprimanded the coachman for doing such a stupid thing. He drove them back to Norman's Grove and they collected the proper collar, leaving the Ward's collar in its place instead.

The nuns continued to travel the length and breadth of the country and on one occasion they were down in County Waterford.

It so happened that, in this big house in County Waterford, a young girl forgot to bring up the jug of water. The nuns rang the bell for someone to come up, and requested the jug of water. The girl ran down the stairs to the kitchen and said to the cook, 'They want a jug of boiling water, I forgot to bring it up.' She brought up the jug of water and – being young and inexperienced – she didn't bother to knock on the door. She ran into the room with the water, put it down, got a surprise, and rushed downstairs to tell the cook that she had run into the room and that one of the nuns was there and she was shaving herself with a big razor.

The owner of the house – who happened to be a justice of the peace – was told about it. He told the police that he had his suspicions about these two and they were questioned and arrested.

It was discovered that they were not nuns at all but a man and wife dressed as nuns, who had kept all of the money for themselves. Of course, the coachman was in on it too. They got a very severe sentence and the case was recorded in the papers, around one hundred years ago.

At the end of the horse stable, there's an arch with double gates that goes out into the haggard. The archway had four square holes at the top of the wall. When they needed to pack wool into the big wool bags, they put two wooden beams into these holes. Ropes were tied to the top corners of the wool pack. The other ends of the four ropes were tied around a stone and the four ropes were thrown over the wooden beams, two ropes over each. That kept the wool pack stretched open, so there was plenty of room for the wool, which was thrown in from the ground.

The bag would have been suspended about a foot from the ground. In order to pack the wool down, one man climbed down from the horse-stable loft door and into the bag. By walking on the wool he'd be able to get a lot more fleeces into the bag. They could have used a boy, but it was usually a small man, because you wanted somebody with a bit of weight in him.

When the bag contained as much wool as it could hold, it was let down to the ground, the four stones were taken out and the flap on the wool sack was sewn shut. In my time it was always Mick Phoenix who sewed the bag shut. He was a very good man to sew and he had a thatch-ing needle for the job. He threaded the twine and when it was done the bag was rolled into the barn, which was at the other side of the archway.

The wool was kept in the barn for a week, or less. It might be gone the next day, because they were anxious to get rid of it: they never want-ed it to get damp by lying on a clay floor. You would be cut in price for having damp wool, because it weighed much more than dry wool.

The bags were rolled up on boards into a cart, one on the bottom and two on top. We'd send six of these bags to the wool merchants, with each pack holding forty or fifty fleeces. They were brought into wool merchants in Dublin, weighed, sold, and you were paid for them there and then.

The sorting of the wool was interesting, because the sorter would have done a number of years' training, usually in Scotland or England. He knew the fibres of the wool and he sorted it very quickly. As two or three men threw the wool onto the table, he just pulled out a fibre and said 'B, C, K, S, T'. Whether it was a male sheep, a female sheep, an Oxford Down, a Suffolk, a Romney Marsh, a Horny, it didn't matter, he could judge it just by the feel of it on his fingers, and the wool would be sent off to different jobs.

If it was all Horny, then it was going for carpets or soldiers blankets, because you couldn't dye it, on account of some of the sheep being brown, others being grey, others being grey and white, and some of them brown and grey.

Supposing you had fifty or sixty Galway sheep, he would say 'P' or 'T' or whatever. But out of those he might pick three that were cross-bred, which might have had a slight touch of the Roscommon, as they called it. They were all thrown on one side. It's difficult for an ordinary person to know the difference between a Galway and a Roscommon lamb, although one is slightly bigger than the other and there is a slight difference in the wool.

You had the type of person – of course it didn't happen here – who always put a few large stones into the fleece in order to increase the weight of the pack. I saw it happening myself and it was usually very embarrassing. The wool merchants unpacked the wool while you were present and when the stone was thrown out onto the wooden floor it made a loud bang. The merchant went over, took out the stone and held it up to the man, so it didn't do him any good anyway, in terms of the price he got for his wool.

There were other fellows who believed in packing wool on a wet day, so that there was plenty of water in it. That didn't work because when the wool merchant saw that the wool was damp, he didn't pay anything like the correct price for it.

That's only by-the-by, it didn't happen here, where they were terribly particular about it. There'd be a row here if even a blade of grass or a bit of straw got into the wool, because you wanted to have top-quality wool and to get the top price for it.

The house adjoining the barn was the storehouse. Many years ago, the corn was kept in stacks and was brought into the barn to be flayed, with a flail. The flail was a whip with three leather tongs on it, and the man beat the corn out of the straw.

It took him ages, but it was his job. If he wasn't one of the men who worked in the place, it would be a man who specialised in that sort of work. You might see him at it for months. After he flayed it, the corn was put into bags. The straw that was left was thrown through a window that connected the the storehouse and the barn. There were a few men in the barn, who gathered it and built it up.

The straw was fed to cattle and was used for thatching, for bedding, or anything else it was suitable for. The thatching straw was kept separately, because it was a different type of straw. They used the best straw for feeding. It was the lighter straw, which had more grass in it.

The coarsest straw was used for bedding. It was used to bed down sixty stall-fed short-horned heifers in Nuttstown. These heifers were tied by the neck to the mangers and given turnips, hay and corn. The last of them were sold in Dublin around 17 March when they were four years old and weighed around eleven hundredweight. Because they were in the house for three or four months, they would have made a considerable amount of manure and used a lot of straw.

The straw could also be sold in Dublin, to a private corn factor. It was brought into the city by two men bringing four loads. Most of the straw was delivered to yards on the north side of the city.

If the four loads were sold to two different men, then one load was delivered by a porter. These porters spent two days of the week delivering hay and straw and one day driving cattle from the cattle market to the boat. Each man was paid a fixed amount according to the distance he had to travel. Then he brought the empty cart to an arranged place where all three of the men met.

The men from Gunnocks were free to refuse to deliver the straw to an unsuitable place, such as Blackrock, or Dundum, or any place that was too far out of town. They would also refuse if they got no help from the buyer and had to put it in by themselves, from a ladder, through a small window into a loft.

Another use for the straw was to enter a contract with a dairy man to supply him with straw once or twice in the week for free. Then they'd take the manured straw back from his yard each week and use it as fertiliser.

The snag with this system was that when fodder was dear, the dairy men didn't put the straw under the cows, they fed it to them instead. When the carts went for the manure, all they got was slurry, which could not be loaded in a cart. To get over this problem, they got a watering can with a rose sprinkler and filled it with paraffin oil. When the cart was loaded, the clean straw was sprinkled with oil. The cows would not eat the straw, which meant that when the men went for manure, there was plenty left in the yard.

However, the thought crossed my mind that if a match was dropped on the straw, the men might go for the manure and find neither manure nor cows. It was because of the danger of fire that an order was brought in allowing only one week's supply of hay or straw to be kept in city yards.

As things progressed, the Wards moved away from the flail and built a grinding machine outside in the yard. It was a big heavy iron machine. The machine was worked by three horses, who walked around in a circle, turning several very large cog wheels. It was fed from outside but the machine deposited the threshed wheat in the barn.

The grinding machine must have cost quite a lot of money at the time, because the ground had to be built up in the yard and they were made of very heavy iron. It also took a fair pull on the horses to keep going around in a circle steadily for quite a length of time.

After that you had the steam threshing mills, which were fired by coal, just the same as the first railway engines. There was coal and water and a big fire in them and they were much quicker and more efficient.

These mills were unable to propel themselves along the road, so horses were used to collect the mill and send it on to the next location. Farmers co-operated to get the mill from farm to farm. If the mill was in Christy Gregan's and if Gunnocks was the next scheduled stop, then two horses would be sent from Gunnocks to Gregan's. Then two horses from Gregan's and two horses from Gunnocks would bring it to Gunnocks. When it was finished in Gunnocks, it might go to Gogan's in Stokestown. Gogan's would send two horses to Gunnocks and would pull the mill to Gogan's with the help of the two Gunnocks horses.

In theory that was grand, but in practice it often didn't work out that way. Supposing the two horses went over to Gregan's place and were tackled to the engine. One of the Gunnocks horses would refuse to work with the Gregan's horses. It was usually the mares that did that. Then she'd get sour and start to jump and there was a danger of breaking the tackle. The horse had to be taken out and they'd have to walk over to Gunnocks to get another horse. Very often, they'd collect a horse from another neighbour and hopefully all four would pull the mill to wherever the next place was.

Off they went and when they had travelled a short distance, one of the horses would get frightened with the noise or the rattle of the mill. They would get very excited and would frighten the others, in which case the others would have to be taken out as well and another horse collected from somewhere else. This did not happen every time, but it happened often. If two horses worked successfully, then the same two would be used the following year, because horses were kept for a long time, much longer than you'd keep a motor car for now.

A lot of hired men followed the mill. They walked along with it and some or all of them were employed at each place.

The last building in the yard was the granary, which was over the store house and which was used for storing grain. The Wards had to store a lot of grain. They threshed it freshly as they needed it, to make sure that they had two or three weeks of it in stock. It was more palatable to the animals when it was freshly threshed.

There's a tiny house under the stone steps that go up to the granary and I often wondered what it was for. It would be too small for a dog. A small dog would fit in it all right, but we didn't keep any small dogs. If we were going to have chicken on a Sunday then the chicken would be put in there on a Tuesday or a Wednesday, to fast for between twenty-four and forty-eight hours before it was killed. Coming up to Christmas we'd have a turkey in it.

The two hay houses were built during my lifetime. Prior to that the hay sheds were wooden, which was very effective. Instead of having metal posts and metal supports to hold up the roof, there were strong wooden supports and wooden posts. They were painted regularly with black naphta and were ideal for the swallows to build their nests on. We used to have a large number of swallows, but once the old hay shed was taken down they left and they didn't come back.

The wooden hay shed had a wooden roof, which was covered in felt. Over the years, new layers of felt were laid on top of the older layers. Then they poured tar over the new felt and scattered fine sand on top of the tar. There was no danger of any leakage getting into the hay.

The calf shed was on the far side of the hay shed. It is a wooden structure with a corrugated iron roof. There were three places for suck calves, another place for calves that were about three or four months old, and another for calves that were around six months old.

9

LAURENCE'S CATTLE MARKET DAYS

There are a number of holes in the wall between the old cowhouse and the loft. When the cattle were going to the market on a Wednesday night, they were brought down before dark and left in that corner of the yard. Wooden bars were put across between the shed and the loft, along with a couple of poles, to pen them. It was a temporary structure that could be taken down the next day but was secure enough to keep the cattle between the yard gate and the lodge. There was a pond at the end of the yard, which had drinking water, and they could lie down if they wanted to.

If there was one man going to the market, then he brought ten cattle. You wouldn't ask them to bring eleven unless there was some special reason for it. They didn't like the idea of being asked to bring eleven; they brought the recognised number, which was ten.

The men went home early the evening before the market. They had their sleep and their tea and came back at around eleven o'clock, to start off for the Dublin cattle market with the cattle.

It took around five hours to walk the cattle to the market and it was impressed upon the men that the cattle were to be walked in quietly. The cattle were inclined to run fast until they got near Clonee and then they eased off. One of the men – usually Jack Hynes – brought a bicycle as far as Clonee, so that they could keep up with them in case they ran up the Dunboyne or the Clonsilla road.

The Kerry men who had land in this part of the country had a much lighter type of a beast. They wouldn't start their journey as early, but they'd be anxious to be in at the same time as the others. They wanted to get by other herds on the road, so they'd shout at people in front, 'Keep in out of that' or 'Pull down a side road and let us pass'. Not only did they have lighter, quicker cattle, but a lot of them kept bulls, which could be very wicked.

The men with cattle coming from Kilcloon, Dunshaughlin, Ratoath and the intervening places used to stop in Clonee. McWilliams public house had a special forty-eight-hour 'haymangers' licence to serve drink and food to these men. The men from Gunnocks wouldn't necessarily get anything in the pub, because they had only travelled a mile along the road and had already had their tea. However, they still stopped in Clonee and waited for my uncle's men from Kilcloon, for the men from Nuttstown, and for the Tooles from Ratoath.

The men from Kilcloon had walked eight or nine miles to Clonee, so our men waited for them while my uncle's men got their supper. They travelled together because they were comrades and stayed together the whole way into Dublin. They didn't mix the cattle, because it was easier for them to drive their own lots.

Before the introduction of cars, many of the farmers stayed in Dublin the night before the market. People who lived near Dublin travelled on the morning of the market, setting off before dawn.

On one occasion, one of the Cuffes, who were cousins of my father's, was driving in from Lissenhall to the cattle markets, early in the morning. He was driving his horse and trap in the dark, with candlelit lamps, past his farm in Collinstown.

The Cuffes had a very large number of farms in north County Dublin. They had Lissenhall, Little Lissenhall, the Leighs and Collinstown Airport. They also had the Hill of Feltrim, which has a tower at the top, which used to be for smelting. I think that they owned Skidoo at one time and they had several other places as well as those.

The Cuffes were also cattle salesmen in the Dublin cattle markets, Cuffe and Sons, Limited. My father and my uncles sold cattle with them in Dublin, but the Cuffes also sold cattle for a great number of south-of-Ireland people, mostly from County Limerick and Clare. The Cuffes used to go to Clare to buy their cattle, and many cattle were sent from customers in Clare to be sold in Dublin. This was because one or two of the Cuffes were married to the Frosts, who were a great family in County

111

Clare. They were Welsh originally, but they had big estates around Sixmilebridge, Cratlow and into Ennis.

On this occasion, Cuffe heard a commotion, a man shouting, cursing and using all kinds of abusive language around cattle in a field. He stopped his trap and the man came out to him.

'What's wrong with you?' Cuffe said to him.

'Ah, bad luck to the careless people who own this place,' he said. 'They left the gate open and my nine heifers are after getting into the field and I can't get them out.'

Cuffe agreed to give him a hand and stood on the road, helping the man to get his cattle out of the field. The man thanked him, he shut the gate, and then Cuffe went off into the market.

He didn't realise what had happened until he got home in the evening and the herd from his farm in Collinstown told him that he was missing nine heifers off the land. Whether or not the man knew who Cuffe was, he got him to help him to steal his own nine heifers.

Men came to market from all over the country and stayed in the various hotels throughout the city, which catered mostly for the cattle men. The south-of-Ireland men stayed at the Four Courts Hotel, because they could get off the train at Sean Heuston Station and either walk or take the outside car to the hotel. In the morning, they hired a jarvey or an outside car and drove up to the cattle market.

My father and I always stayed at the Gresham, which also catered for the market men and kept their market clothes for them. The Gresham had early-morning tea for the market men, and the tram stopped at the door, on the opposite side of O'Connell Street. There were special trams which were just for the men going to the market. The first left at half-five and the next one left at six o'clock.

My uncles Michael and Patrick stopped in Vaughan's Hotel in Parnell Square, which wasn't anything as nice as the Gresham. My uncle liked to go down to the monastery in Dominick Street, which was behind the hotel. They took the tram from Findlater's Church or from Nelson's Pillar in O'Connell Street.

The disadvantage of Vaughan's Hotel during troubled times was that Michael Collins used to stay in it. The Black and Tans, the Auxiliaries and ordinary British soldiers used to raid it, so my uncle was often pulled out of his bed while his room was searched. On one occasion he had to go down onto the street, because they told him that they were going to burn down the hotel.

They never caught Collins of course, because the night porter and the day porter were faithful followers of his and he was always tipped off in time. As soon as the Crossley tenders arrived on the scene, he escaped out the back, got out into Dominick Street and was never caught.

Commandant Sean Boylan, who lived at the railway bridge in Dunboyne, used to stay in the Gresham Hotel when he was on the run from the British. On one occasion, my father was walking up the stairs to his bedroom when he saw Commandant Boylan coming down towards him. He was about to give him some salutation, but luckily Boylan had seen him coming and pressed his finger to his lips. My father knew that he should pretend not to recognise him and they passed each other without recognition of any kind.

Patrick's wife, my Aunt Ita, was a very fastidious person and used to say, 'Oh, I wish Patrick would stay someplace else, he always brings back a flea with him from Vaughan's Hotel.' I used to wonder why he only brought home just one flea and never two.

When Vaughan's was burned, my two uncles moved to Barry's Hotel, on Great Denmark Street. When the Gresham was burned down, my father moved to the Hibernian Hotel on Dawson Street, taking an outside car from there to the market.

The Dublin cattle market on the North Circular Road was built to replace the old cattle-and-sheep market in Smithfield. The new market covered sixty acres and accommodated up to six thousand cattle. It was – to the best of my knowledge – the biggest livestock market in Europe. The new market, which also sold pigs and milking cows, may even have been the biggest livestock market in the world.

People who sold the cattle in the market were known as 'standholders'. Standholders were usually farmers who bought cattle in fairs and sold them in the Dublin market; the only place that held a market rather than a fair. The Ward faily were typical standholders. Each standholder had a certain number of pens. We had enough pens for forty cattle, but there were other standholders who had enough pens for five or six hundred cattle.

Standholders also had small wooden offices and paid a small fee to the Dublin Corporation for the use of the office and the electric lighting. Some of them had a clerk, while others did the work themselves. The buyers paid for their cattle in the offices, which were used to store the ropes from week to week.

A number of the cattle stands were owned by Protestants, who sold practically all Protestant cattle. The Catholics sold practically all Catholic cattle, but both Catholics and Protestants got on really well together. We helped each other and tipped each other off about anything that they might want to know about so-and-so, who was buying a certain class of cattle, and so on.

The cattle were kept in steel pens, which held ten large cattle. The pens were wonderfully well constructed and very well kept: they were painted every year and the cattle stood on cobbled stone, which was three inches higher at the top of the pen that it was at the bottom. A channel ran along the bottom of the pen, into which the urine and droppings fell, and there were manholes along the channels into which they were swept.

Once the cattle were in the pens, they were tied by the neck with ropes. Even though most cattle – in those days – had horns, anybody that would tie them by the horns was seen as a pretty poor type of a person; no reputable person would tie them by the horns.

The cattle were tied by men known as 'pen men', who were absolute experts at their job. The pen men didn't see the cattle until they were driven onto the stand. They'd ask how many cattle you had and how you wanted them tied. You'd tell them that you had twenty cattle and wanted ten tied in each pen. The pen man would look them over quickly and would put them in order, the tallest beast at the top, and then the next tallest, down to the smallest one at the end.

While two men held the cattle up to the pen, a third man put a rope around its neck and tied it around the bar. It took him thirty seconds or less. The rope was pulled in such as a way that if the beast pulled, it did not hurt its neck in any way; the pull was on the iron bar of the pen.

The biggest markets were in October and November, and any cattle that couldn't be accommodated in the market were kept in yards all around Prussia Street, Aughrim Street, Manor Street and Stonybatter. When a few pens were sold, they were sent down to the yards and an equal number were brought up from the yard to be tied in the pens. If they were only to be kept for an hour before being brought down to the boat, they were kept on what was known as the 'waste ground', which was part of the cattle market.

The market opened at around two o'clock in the morning. Our cattle were always in by five o'clock and were tied up and settled in their places by half past five. We hadn't a pen man, we had our own men who walked in with the cattle: Christy and Jack Hynes from the Gunnocks, Dick Garry from Kilcloon, and Peter Rooney from Nuttstown.

Christy and Jack tied up the cattle, and they were very good at it. There was a man by the name of Kennedy who used to feed a lot of cattle and who couldn't stand the way the Dublin drovers tied the cattle.

He always said, 'I want to get those two nice boys you have up here, those two, Jack and Christy, to come down and tie the cattle for me.' They would – on occasion – go down and tie his cattle.

Once the cattle were tied, they went into the office and laid down for a couple of hours of sleep. Then they went down to various places in Stonybatter and had their breakfast in the 'ating house that belonged to Miss Doggett, who was a native of Navan.

There were any number of these places, which catered for anybody who needed to be fed: buyers, sellers, drovers, pen men and country men. Each of them regarded their own 'ating house as better than the next. There were some very nice places, run by widows or by women who hadn't married, and they all had their own clientele.

My father used to go to an 'ating house in Prussia Street. One day he was in the market and a man asked him where he was going.

'Ah, I'm going down to get my breakfast.'

'Where do you get it?'

'Ah, I get it in Miss So-and-So on Prussia Street.'

'Oh, I wouldn't eat my breakfast there.'

My father wondered why. You'd hear all sorts of stories: that the steaks in such-and-such an establishment were cut from horses, which had been discovered when a fellow walked into a bedroom by mistake and found the shod leg of a horse on the bed.

'I'll tell you why. There's men comes up from the south of Ireland, Tipperary and Kilkenny, in the springtime of the year. They're that holy that if you were any way grazey, they'd ate you.'

My father never had any experience like that: he never ate horse meat and nobody ever tried to eat him. In later years, he changed to the City Arms, which is where he brought me, and I never went anywhere else.

10

Laurence and the War of Independence

I am now going to record my father's part in the national movement, leading up to the setting up of our own government under the Free State.

When the struggle for independence began after the rebellion in 1916, my father considered that, as a nationalist, he should give up his posts as a justice of the peace and as a member of the Grand Jury. He went to see Sean Boylan, who was a very prominent man in the national movement and who had a huge area under him. Commandant Boylan was the father of Sean Boylan, who is the current coach of the Meath GAA team.

He told Boylan that he thought that he should give up these posts, but Boylan told him to stay. He said that we needed to have some of our people on these boards, people who would favour the nationalist cause.

My father said that he would stay on the boards if Boylan wished, but that there was a chance that he would be shot for keeping his position on the boards.

'You need have no fear of that,' said Boylan. 'You will be very well looked after.'

That turned out to be very true. All through the troubled times – which were pretty bad – we as a family were well looked after at the Gunnocks. We never had any robberies or trouble of any kind, and we attribute that to Commandant Sean Boylan.

My father was at the Roscommon fair on Easter Monday, when the Dublin uprising began in 1916. He had bought some cattle in Roscommon, which Mattie Ward had loaded onto the train. Mattie

OHMS
June 27, 1916
Home Office
Whitehall
SW

Dear Sir,
    The *Advisory Committee*, sitting to consider the cases of deported Irishmen, have just had before them the case of John Boylan of Dunboyne, County Meath.
    He has asked the Committee to write to you, as one of his references, and the Committee would be very grateful if you would, as soon as possible, send them a brief account of what you know about him.
    I enclose franked envelope for your reply.
    Yours faithfully,
    Paul M. Frauche

Laurence Ward Esq JP
Gunnocks
Clonee
County Dublin
Ireland

travelled to Clonsilla in the guard's van, unloaded the cattle, and walked them back the few miles to Gunnocks.

My father, who was sixty-six at the time, continued on to Broadstone Station, from where he could catch a train to Dunboyne. He was told that there were no trains running to Dunboyne and that there were no trains travelling at all, because there had been some disturbance in the city.

We had no phone at Gunnocks, so he decided that he would send a telegram to Clonee to tell them that he was coming. Then he found that the telegraph wasn't working either, so he decided to walk up to Doyle's corner, in Phibsborough. In those days, Doyle's pub belonged to people named Dunphy, whom he knew very well.

As he walked up, he met somebody and asked them why there were no trams running. They told him that nothing was running at all and that they'd heard that a soldier and his horse had been shot down in Parnell Square. He didn't know what to think of it.

He called to Dunphys, who told him that they knew a man with a dairy float, who would leave him home as he travelled out to Meath with his milk churns. However, the man with the milk float didn't want to go to Meath in case he wouldn't be allowed back into the city afterwards. In the end he agreed to drop him to Clonee. He dropped my father in Clonee and told him to walk the last mile himself, since he was anxious to get back into the city before they closed it off. At that stage, neither of them knew that the 'disturbance' was a rising that had taken place in the city.

After the Rising, Sean Boylan was imprisoned because of his position. My father, because of his position, had a certain amount of influence over the British authorities. He interceded for him, and Sean Boylan never forgot that.

During the Troubles, the British authorities went around collecting all of the privately owned guns, because they didn't want them falling into the hands of the Sinn Féiners.

My father went to Commandant Sean Boylan and offered him a double-barrelled shotgun and a rifle, because he wanted Boylan to have them before the British authorities came to take them. However, Boylan refused the offer of the guns.

In due course, two British army officers called to the house on a Thursday, when my father was at the market. They were very English and very polite to my mother, and explained that they had come to get the guns. My mother told them that they were locked in my father's office and that he was away at the market. If they insisted on collecting them, they could break in the door of the office. They said that they wouldn't do such a thing and that they would return for them some other day.

The next time they called, my father was there. They took possession of the guns, wrote down the particulars of each, and gave him a receipt for them. After the treaty was signed, people whose guns had been taken up were at liberty to retrieve them from the barracks. My father went in with a receipt and got back both the shotgun and the rifle. Each had been numbered with permanent paint, but they were in perfect condition.

In 1914, the third and final Home Rule bill was passed by the British government and was then shelved for the duration of the First World War. More than one hundred thousand Irish men signed up to fight for Britain in the war, encouraged by Irish Parliamentary Party leaders in Westminister.

However, over the four years of the war, the political mood in Ireland changed radically. This was partly because of fears that the British would introduce conscription in Ireland and partly due to the rise of Sinn Féin, whose political fortunes rose rapidly in the aftermath of the armed uprising in 1916. From 1916 until 1921, the British struggled to control Ireland as Irish nationalists fought to establish an independent republic. By the end of the war, a new generation of political leaders had emerged, including Michael Collins.

Michael Collins was born in Cork in 1890, the eighth child of a prosperous farmer. He joined the British civil service when he was sixteen years old and moved to London to work in the postal service. He returned to Ireland to fight in the 1916 rebellion and was interned in Frongoch. After being released from Frongoch, he returned to Ireland as one of the leaders of Sinn Féin and the IRA.

In the 1918 elections, the Irish Parliamentary Party was all but annihilated by Sinn Féin, which won two-thirds of the votes outside of unionist-dominated north-east Ulster. Sinn Féin refused to take their seats in Westminster and set up a parliament in Dublin, called Dáil Éireann. After the local elections, Sinn Féin also gained control of the county councils, which switched their allegiance to the Dáil. The Sinn Féin government set up their own court service, policing and prison service.

The British attempted to kill off the Dáil by introducing a Home Rule bill, which established two parliaments in Ireland, one for the nationalist-dominated twenty-six counties and one for the unionist-dominated counties in the north-east.

They also brought in reinforcements to back up the Royal Irish Constabulary, which was overwhelmed by the IRA. These 'Black and Tans' were former British soldiers, many of whom were veterans of World War One, some of whom were shell-shocked, and most of whom were completely unfit for policing duties. The British government also recruited Auxiliaries, former British army officers who were seen as the elite anti-IRA military force.

Both British military forces alienated the public with their brutality. They burned down towns, shot innocent civilians and torched the creameries belonging to the Irish Co-operative Society. In retaliation, the IRA started burning the homes of former landlords, many of whom had already fled to England, fearing for their safety.

I had only one personal experience of the British military. My father, mother and I were coming home from Dublin in the brougham, driven by Mattie Ward. When we came to Loughsallagh crossroads, there was a road check that consisted of about twelve armed British soldiers on each side of the road. They indicated to Mattie that he should drive the brougham into the centre of the road, at which point they surrounded it. All four of us got down onto the road and were searched. Then they searched the brougham. There was nothing to find in the brougham, so we were beckoned to continue onwards.

We had a grand black working horse, which was around four years old. On a particular day, he had been ploughing as part of a pair, and the workman was standing between the two horses, leading them out for the night at the back of Mattie Ward's house.

When they got up to Floody's Harrow, a piece of land along the road, a large convoy of Black and Tans, under the command of a British officer, drove by in Crossley tenders. The Black and Tans were all terribly drunk, because they were after burning down the town of Trim, or a large part of it. In those days, horses were not used to the noise of motor cars or engines. This young horse was frightened and he swung out onto the road, and his hind legs were broken by a Crossley tender.

The workman came back to the yard, accompanied by the British officer. It was just before dark, and father came down to speak to the officer. The officer, who had also a great deal of drink taken, was extremely polite and apologised for the accident.

'Now,' he said. 'Have no worries about it whatsoever, you'll be paid full compensation for this horse.'

He wrote out a receipt document to say that the horse had been damaged due to the negligence of the driver and that it had to be destroyed.

'Have no hesitation,' he said. 'Come into the barracks and you'll be paid.'

He also said that he knew a great deal about horses and offered to shoot the horse. My father said that he would prefer to get Mister Magee, the veterinary surgeon, to come over to shoot the horse. The officer was terribly polite, and away he went.

121

Father was not going to lose the price of his horse, so he decided that he would go into the barracks to get paid. That was an extremely risky thing to do, because anybody seen going up to a barracks would have been regarded as somebody who was giving information to the British military about the Sinn Féiners. He could quite easily have been picked off by a sniper when he left the barracks. However, he was a determined man and he decided to go to the barracks.

The gates of the barracks were very closely guarded by the military, but it happened that the policeman on the gate was Mister Bonham, who was married to one of the Beltons. After Bonham left the force, he and his wife set up their own public house in Clonee, where the Grasshopper pub is now located.

Bonham saluted my father, who explained the position to him. Bonham escorted him to the officer's room, where he claimed £75 for the horse. That was a good price for a horse at that time, but he was paid there and then.

Robberies were rife wholesale during the Black and Tan regime. A number of their members had been left out of prison to join the Black and Tans, and they deserted when they got to Ireland, taking up robbery instead.

Quite a number of Irish people also took up robbery during that period, so when the provisional government took over from the British, they had to introduce strong measures to put a stop to the wholesale robbery, murder and shooting that was taking place.

The cat-o'-nine-tails was introduced, and the first individual to be given this punishment was a man who worked as a signal man at Dunboyne railway station. He was not actually from this part of the country, but he and one other man were given the cat-o'-nine-tails, and it stopped the robberies at once.

The Sinn Féiners set up their own courts, which weren't legally binding until the provisional government took over from the British. To support the courts, the Sinn Féiners needed jails, into which they could put the criminals for their crimes, many of which would not be terribly serious.

My father rarely met Commandant Boylan during the troubles, because he was incognito and was always on the run. The late John Kelly of Sarney, who was a Sinn Féin representative, came to my father and told him that they wanted Norman's Grove, for use as a jail. My father demurred: he didn't see why he should hand over Norman's Grove, when he didn't know what way it would be used. He told Jack that he wasn't prepared to do such a thing.

'Well,' said Jack. 'What are we going to do if you don't give it?'

My father knew, by the way he said it, that if he didn't give it, then it would have been taken.

'Oh, very well,' he said. 'If that's the way you feel, then you can have it.'

Norman's Grove was already rented to a British judge called Rippton Curran, who had spent his career in India. After he retired, he moved to Ireland with his wife, who was related to the Wilkinsons of Rathbeggan.

The Black and Tans raided Norman's Grove on one occasion when the Rippton Currans were living there. It would appear that somebody told the Black and Tans – as a joke, or to annoy them – that there were arms hidden in the secret passage out in the lawn.

They searched the whole place and the Rippton Currans were very upset. They didn't know where the secret passage was, so the Black and Tans went down to Mrs Rogers, an old woman who was living in the lodge. They came into her house, put a gun to her head, frightened the life out of her, and told her to bring them to the secret passage so that they could find the guns.

She directed them to the passage, which is over near the turret. They took up one or two of the big flagstones, went down the steps and found that the tunnel was full of water, as it always is. Then they left.

Nevertheless, the Rippton Currans loved Norman's Grove, and Mrs Rippton Curran said to my father, 'I hope you will leave us on so that I can die here.' That wasn't to be, because the Sinn Féiners gave them a week to get out of the country.

Rippton Curran's political leanings would have been towards Britain, but I wouldn't imagine that he was able to give information to the British authorities. He was quite old and so was his wife.

I was with my father in Greystones when we got a telegram – there were very few phones in those days and most of the wires had been cut – to say that they would be leaving within a week and that they wanted to settle up. Father and I went home on the train to see the Rippton Currans, who were terribly upset.

When they were gone, the Sinn Féiners took Norman's Grove over as a jail. They put a number of men into the house, but I've no idea how many. We always kept away from these places, because you didn't want to be accused of giving information. If people thought that you were giving information then you'd be shot, or your place would be burned, or your hay would be burned or your cattle maimed.

They occupied the place for some time and only one man escaped from it as far as I know. He managed to open one of the upstairs windows and jumped down into a shrub that was growing at the end of the house, as you go into the yard.

The Sinn Féiners and their prisoners did no real damage. The men picked pieces out of the marble fireplaces as they were sitting around with nothing to do; they had no books or anything. If any real damage had been done then my father could have claimed from the provisional government. He never claimed, because the damage was very small.

It was very difficult to travel during that time. Almost all of the road bridges over rivers and railways had been blown up. People often brought a strong board with them to cover the hole in the bridge. They laid the board over the hole so that they could drive a cart across the bridge using the board and the remains of the road.

The bridge going over the River Tolka into Clonee had two huge holes in it. One of them had a big furze bush stuck in it, but the other one was open. When you were driving cattle into Dublin, the cattle would jostle each other and one of them would be knocked into the hole and would fall into the river. The cattle were unhurt and emerged after walking downstream to Summerseat, which at that point belonged to the Garnet family.

On one occasion, my father was travelling to the Carlow fair on 27 March. Mattie Ward was driving him in the pony and trap to get the three o'clock train from Dunboyne into the city. Then he'd travel down to Heuston Station to get the train to Carlow. On the way from Loughsallagh to the station, they met my uncle Michael and my cousin Joe, who were driving along in a new Ford car. The Staffordstown Wards were some of the first people to get a car.

They said, 'Are you going to Carlow?'

'I am,' he said.

'So are we. You may as well get into the car with us and we'll drive straight down to Kingsbridge.' Heuston Station was known as Kingsbridge in those days. My father supposed that he might as well, so he got into the car.

Somewhere between Blanchardstown and Dublin the car broke down. In those days, nobody knew anything about them, and unless you knew something about them you couldn't get parts and it was a lot of bother. After some hours, my cousin got the car started, and they continued on to Kingsbridge.

The train was already gone by that point and there were no more trains to Carlow that evening; the furthest they could get to was Kildare, from where they hoped to get a car.

My father felt that it would have been far better if he had gone on by himself, but he couldn't do anything about it at that point.

It was dark by the time they got to Kildare, but there was a motor car at the station. They asked the driver to bring them to Carlow.

'Oh no, I wouldn't think of driving the car to Carlow in the dark, the Black and Tans are all about,' he said. 'It could be commandeered or any one of us could be shot.'

So they had to stay in Kildare for the night and the driver collected them at daylight to drive them to Carlow.

In order to catch Sinn Féiners, the Black and Tans used to block off each end of a street in Dublin and search everybody in the street as they went out at either end. Each of the houses on the street would also be searched. You always felt very uncomfortable because there was always a danger that somebody might fire on the Black and Tans, police or army, and that you might get shot.

My father had a friend, an extremely nice man by the name of Mister Fagan, who was a farmer in County Dublin. Fagan was caught in one of these street searches one day when he was in Dublin. They ran their hands down through his trouser pockets and then he passed through.

When he moved on, he put his hand in his pocket and found that his wallet had been taken. He knew that it had happened when he was going into the street, so he waited until the search was over and went back to the commanding officer.

'Look here,' he said to him. 'I had a wallet when I was going into the street, and after I was searched, the wallet had disappeared.'

'Oh,' said the officer. 'That's a very serious matter, a very serious matter. Do you think you would know the man who searched you?'

'Yes,' said Fagan. 'I would know him.'

'Well,' he said. 'I'll have them lined up along the street. You go along the footpath and point out the man who searched you.'

That was an extremely dangerous thing to do, because they could take it out on you afterwards. Fagan was very quiet, but he went along and pointed out the man to the officer.

The officer said to the man, 'This gentleman says that before you searched him he had a wallet in his pocket and after you searched him the wallet was gone. How do you account for that?'

'I'm sorry sir, it was just a joke,' he said, and took out half a dozen wallets from his pocket.

'Look here, Jones,' said the officer. 'No more of these jokes, they're just not the thing to do.'

So you can see how you were up against a very unscrupulous crowd.

My Uncle Patrick at Nuttstown was robbed twice, although very little was taken. Two Black and Tans came to him on one particular occasion. These men were deserters or robbers who had probably been in jail in England for robbing, but they took it up again when they came over here.

They called to Nuttstown when it was dark and said that they were there to search for guns. My uncle let them in; he didn't know if they would have broken in or fired on him, or goodness knows what.

My Aunt Ita had some lovely jewellery and rings that she kept under the mattress. She stayed in bed as they searched all around. They went upstairs to the bedroom and ordered her out of the bed, very politely. She refused to get out of the bed, because she didn't want them searching under the mattress. They may have suspected that, but they didn't force her to get out of bed, and none of her jewellery was taken.

However, she used to have a very good hunting mare called Cora. When Cora died, my aunt had her hooves hollowed out and covered in silver. She put a label onto it and she kept it on the table as an ornament. The Black and Tans decided that they would take that.

My uncle was a very quiet, harmless sort of a man, but he persuaded them that it would upset his wife very much if they took the silver hooves.

He suggested that they take something else instead. I don't know if they did take anything else; they went off without the silver shoes and that was that.

The Auxiliary police were put in after most of the RIC had resigned; the Royal Irish Constabulary were mostly Irish and weren't able to control the country during this period. Many of them resigned for fear of being shot or out of sympathy for the nationalist cause. They were really no better than the Black and Tans, but they had a different job. I remember one Auxiliary who had the job of directing traffic at the top of Grafton Street and Nassau Street. He was a magnificent-looking man and he used to direct traffic with a revolver. He kept the gun in his right hand and directed cars to go or stop or whatever he wanted them to do. A fine-looking man, he was easy to pick off; he was shot dead from the window of a nearby restaurant.

My Uncle Michael travelled to every fair in Tullow, County Carlow. He used to stop in a private house in the centre of the town, which was run by two old ladies, and he was the only person they took in. He was extremely deaf, so there wasn't any point in knocking on his door; he always woke in time for the fair.

On this occasion, he went downstairs in the morning expecting that they would have the kettle boiling for him. They weren't up, so he wondered where they were. There was an awful smell of smoke about the place, so he opened the door and looked out. As far as he could see, the whole street was filled with smoke, burning and crackling. The houses at each end of the town were on fire.

There were no people or cattle in the street, so he walked to the edge of the town and saw all of the people, who had evacuated because the Black and Tans had set fire to the town.

In May 1921, the British held an election for the twenty-six-county Home Rule parliament that it had established. Sinn Féin contested the election and won 124 seats, while the Unionists won four. In the election for the Northern Ireland parliament, the Unionists won forty seats, Sinn Féin six seats, and the IPP six seats.

By this point both sides were open to negotiations. The British government was losing support for its policies in Ireland, both in Britain and internationally, and were left with the choice of either waging an all-out war against the IRA or holding talks with the Sinn Féin. The Irish public was war-weary and wanted peace. The IRA was down to its last few weeks of ammunition, and Collins believed that it could not last much longer.

Dáil Éireann sent Collins and Arthur Griffith, the founder of Sinn Féin, to negotiate with the British. The resulting Anglo-Irish Treaty gave Ireland Dominion status, along the same lines as Canada and South Africa, and was presented by Collins as a 'stepping stone to freedom'.

It was also agreed that north-east Ulster could stay outside the Irish state, but that a boundary commission would be set up to shift the border at a later date, to bring the more nationalist areas into the new Irish state.

To some extent, Collins and Griffith had been out-negotiated by Churchill and Lloyd George. On another level, the Treaty was a huge achievement for the delegates, since it gave Ireland control of its own finances and foreign policy.

The Treaty was debated in the Dáil, with its opponents focusing on the fact that it fell short of full independence and that the members of the Dáil would have to take an oath of allegiance to the King of England. The partition of Ireland was assumed to be temporary arrangement and was hardly mentioned during the debates. The Dáil passed the treaty, with sixty-four votes in favour and fifty-seven against. The electorate endorsed this Dáil vote in the 1922 elections, in which pro-Treaty Sinn Féin won fifty-eight seats; Labour seventeen; Farmers seven; Independents seven; and Unionists four. All of these groups supported the Treaty. Anti-Treaty Sinn Féin candidates won thirty-five seats.

The strong showing by the Farmers Party, Independent Party and Labour showed that the Treaty was not the only pressing question of the day and that people wanted life to return to normal.

Arthur Griffith and Michael Collins took on the task of setting up and running the new state, while Éamon de Valera, the President of the Dáil, chose not to accept the results of the Dáil vote or the elections. When forced to choose sides in the Civil War, he supported the efforts of the anti-Treaty IRA to overthrow the new state.

The country was soon gripped by a Civil War between the Free State army and the anti-Treaty elements of the IRA. During the war, Griffith died of a heart attack and Collins died in an ambush.

The government, now led by W. T. Cosgrave and Kevin O'Higgins, introduced an Emergency Powers Act, which allowed it sweeping powers to end lawlessness and *authorised the death penalty for a wide range of crimes. The anti-Treaty IRA had limited public support and fared poorly against the Free State Army. Towards the end of the war, many anti-Treaty IRA members were executed by the army in brutal and dubious circumstances.*

Throughout the War of Independence and Civil War, the live cattle export trade with Britain continued without interruption.

The 'luck penny' was a standard practice in the Dublin cattle market. The idea was that for every hundred pounds' worth of cattle a man bought from you in the markets, you gave him five shillings. At the fairs in the countryside, it was usually two shillings, or two shillings and sixpence. If the fellow only gave you a shilling, or a shilling and sixpence, you thought pretty badly of him, and so would the other sellers.

On one occasion, during the troubled times, my father's cousin Laurence of Fieldstown was taking a taxi up to the train in Ballinasloe. He had bought around twenty cattle off a man called James Cooke. Cooke, who was a very unpopular man, wouldn't give Laurence the proper luck penny. The other men in the car were saying 'Come on Laurence, we'll all miss the train', so Laurence put his pride in his pocket and got into the car, annoyed at being badly treated by Cooke. He got in beside the driver of the car, a man who often drove me and who lives down there still.

'Was ould Cooke treating you badly?' he said.

'Ah, yes,' said Laurence. 'What about him!'

'Well now, look here,' said he. 'I'll have that luck penny for you the next fair when you get here.'

He gave Laurence a poke in the side with a revolver.

'I won't be long getting it out of ould Cooke, when I give him a prod of this.'

'Oh no, not at all,' said Laurence. 'Not at all, I wouldn't hear of such a thing, I wouldn't, put that gun away out of that, I wouldn't hear of such a thing as that.'

11

Joe's Cattle Market Days

My first memory of cattle was when I was four years old. My father used to drive through the fields in a pony and trap, with Jem Earley driving the pony, whose name was Dolly. Mary Matthews — who was my nurse at that time — used to bring me along in the trap. On that particular day we were up in the fourteen acres, when I saw a black-horned cow in the field. Speaking to nobody in general, I said, 'That's the cow that gave Joseph milk'.

Now, I was quite right, because I had seen that cow going in and out of the cowhouse. Because she was not in calf, she was put out into the field to fatten.

The next thing I remember took place was when I was nine. My father used to buy cows from an elderly man called Pat Lynch. Pat was a very shrewd Cavan man from Ballyjamesduff, but he always said that he was from 'Balladuff'.

He bought these cows in Cavan, Leitrim and Longford, he put them on the train in Oldcastle and took them off at some of the stations in County Meath. He'd always have nine cows, because that was the full of a wagon. Depending on the size of them, you could put ten bullocks or eleven heifers in a wagon. He would then walk them around to various farms and small fairs, such as Ratoath, Athboy, Trim and Navan. When he sold them, he'd go back and buy more.

On this particular day he arrived in the yard with nine very nice cows, which had been bought in Mohill. He shut the yard gate and kept them down at the pond.

My father had gone away for the morning, but I came out and looked over the cows and thought that they looked very well. I asked Pat the price of them and had a good deal of talk about them. I can't remember if there were any of them that I didn't like, but it's unlikely because he was an exceptionally good judge. When my father came along he bought the cows, but Pat always claimed that I bought the cows, but that isn't quite correct.

Over the years I learned a good deal of things from Pat Lynch. He had a very good manner which went down very well with the men in the fairs. Now these would not be very well-educated men and therefore they liked you to have a joke with them or to remember that they had got married the year before or something like that. I was always good at that and I was also good at why I think is now called psychology. I was able to size up the man very well, so as to know what to say to him and to touch him on a soft point in order to get good value out of him.

Pat was very shrewd, as all the Cavan men were. The people in the fair wanted to know what he gave for an animal so that they could get much the same themselves. He was always very polite about it and non-committal.

One day somebody said to him, 'Ah Mister Lynch, what did you give for the white cow standing above in the corner'.

Pat of course knew well which cow they were talking about, but he would say, 'The white cow? The white cow? Is she white, she is?'

'Ah yes,' said the man. 'She's the white cow standing up in the corner.'

He'd think again and say, 'Ah, I know well the cow you mean, I gave a pound too much for that one.'

Then he'd walk away and it was a nice way of getting out of it.

In the springtime he'd be offered big thin leggy cows in Roscommon, which were known as the Croghan breed. They went out years ago, but they looked as though a small body had been put up on stilts. The man would say, 'Hey Mister Lynch, would you buy that one off me?' Pat would look at her and he'd say, 'How much for the haybarn?' It was a fairly good expression, because these cows were just like the roof on a haybarn, with four long stays underneath.

I remember seeing a number of northern cattle in Tuam one day. They were terribly big and desperately hungry cattle, because they'd only be fed for three months of the winter. They'd really be starved for those three months, they'd be fed hazel rods and things like that. I remember a northern fellow saying to a Tuam man, 'Stand out in front of that bullock'.

The man said, 'What do you want me to stand in front of that bullock for?'

'Do as you're tould,' he told him.

So the country man stood in front of the bullock and the northern fellow lifted up the bullock's tail and says he, 'Ah, it's alright, I just wanted to see could I see you through him, he's that empty.'

I was educated here at Gunnocks by Miss Christina O'Brien, who was my governess. She taught me to read very well and was also quite good at teaching me writing.

One of the other reasons why I learned to read so well was that my father was unable to read by artificial light, because it hurt his eyes. I used to have to read to him by the fire of a winter's evening, maybe for two or three hours. I'd be sitting right here, in this same chair. I liked reading, but some of what he wanted was a bit deep for me; he was terribly keen on Dickens. I wanted to please him, so I used to read a lot for him.

My father and his brothers had been to Castleknock College, which was very much geared towards the farming community in Meath, Kildare and County Dublin. My father and his brothers did not like it, or at least, my father did not like it. My mother prevailed on him to send me to a place called Clongowes; it's a big old barracks of a place up in County Kildare. It was run by priests called Jesuits, or 'Jays' as the boys called them. I believe that it's still there and that it's still run by the Jesuits.

The Jesuits went in for teaching what are called 'the Classics'. They were not interested in any boys that were going on for farming or shopkeeping or business. They were only interested in boys who would shine in the universities, who would get scores of MAs and doctorates and whatever you get in universities. The subjects that were taught were Irish, Latin, geometry and algebra, which were all terribly useless things when you were going out to buy a crooked 'oul bullock or an old cow, so you could see that I certainly was not interested in it, I didn't work at it and I got any amount of beatings with the strap. Bill Healy — who was a very decent man indeed — was the cobbler and he made these straps out of leather. They were ferocious things.

After a few years in Clongowes I had learned nothing and my father took me home. The Ferris boys, who were there with me, hated it the same as I did. They were also taken away by their father and sent to the national school in Clane, County Kildare. They later became very prominent in the cattle trade.

Con Kehely, who at one point was one of the biggest live cattle shippers in the country, wasn't any better at school than the Ferrises or myself, because none of us had any interest in it.

The academic part of Clongowes was not everything. If you were good at rugby or cricket then it didn't matter a button if you never did a bit of academic work. The sporting kind of boys were encouraged; they were specially fed and all that kind of thing. I remember Judge Charlie Conroy, who came up from Connemara where he wouldn't have had much to eat, no more than the ould bullocks that his father used to feed. But the Jesuits certainly fattened Charlie up. He became a judge in the High Court and was a very decent man. It never changed him, even with all of his honours and his doctorate. Charlie was regarded as the worst-dressed judge in the country and certainly it would be hard to find anybody worse dressed.

I remember poor Mattie Ward collecting me from Clongowes for the last time. When he got to the gate he slowed the car down and I spat out onto the avenue.

'Ah,' he said. 'Surely you didn't think that badly of it, wasn't it a grand place.'

'It was an awful hole,' I said. 'That's what it was.'

That's enough about that awful place.

I started going to the market when I left school at the age of seventeen. My father had given up going to markets, because he was heading for eighty years old.

I went every week with my Uncle Michael and my cousin Joe who ran Staffordstown, a farm he rented from Mrs Austen. My Uncle Patrick came along every third week, because he didn't feed as many cattle. They picked me up in their car at Loughsallagh crossroads and we drove to a garage on the North Circular Road.

We'd drive past all of the cattle on their way to the market. Some men were driving cows for the cow market, where dairy cattle were sold, either loose or tied. Patrick Bermingham – who lived in Huntstown House outside Mulhuddart – might have fifty or sixty cows one week, or as many as one hundred and twenty the next. It all depended on how many had calved with him during the week and how many he'd managed to buy throughout the country over the previous week. When I drove through them with my uncle in a car, it would sometimes take three-quarters of a mile to pass them out on the road.

For the first decade after the foundation of the state, the Irish government was led by Cumann na nGaedhael, the pro-Treaty wing of Sinn Féin. The new government steered a steady, sensible course and established a state where everybody was forced to respect the democratic rule of law. However, it lost power in 1932 because it failed to deliver on the social and economic expectations that people had from an independent Irish republic.

In August 1923, Cumann na nGaedhael, led by W. T. Cosgrave and Kevin O'Higgins, won sixty-three seats. Independents won sixteen seats, Farmers fifteen and Labour fourteen. Anti-Treaty Sinn Féin won forty-four seats.

The new government set up an unarmed police force and a courts system. Many civil servants transferred from the British Civil Service, which meant that, in terms of civil administration, there was a smooth transition from the United Kingdom to the new Irish State.

The government steered a steady and conservative path in terms of its economic policy. Although they carried out some land reform, they accepted the economic importance of the cattle export trade and allowed trade with England to continue unimpeded.

They set up the Agricultural Credit Corporation, a state-owned bank, to provide finance for farmers. It established a sugar factory in Carlow to process sugar beet, in an attempt to foster native industry. It commissioned Siemens to build a hydroelectric dam at Ardnacrusha, to provide electricity to the country.

The new government also set about dismantling the Anglo-Irish Treaty and weakening constitutional links with Britain. As the most anti-British member of the Commonwealth, Ireland began to erode Britain's dominance of the British Commonwealth, with the help of South Africa. Once the Statute of Westminster was passed in 1932, establishing legislative equality between all Commonwealth countries, the Irish State was free to leave the Commonwealth if it so chose.

However, the new government suffered a setback in 1924 when the failure of the Boundary Commission meant that Northern Ireland would not be reunited with the rest of the island. Its popularity also suffered because it agreed to continue collecting

134

the Land Annuities from the farmers and paying them to the British government.

As a result of the Great Depression in 1929, which had a severe effect upon the economies of industrialised countries like Britain, the price of cattle began to fall, and unemployment grew from 21,000 to 31,000.

In 1932, Fianna Fáil – formerly the anti-Treaty wing of Sinn Féin – won seventy-two seats against Cumann na nGaedhael's fifty-seven. Initially, there were fears that Cumann na nGaedhael would refuse to hand over power to their Civil War enemies. However, the leadership of Cumann na nGaedhael, true to their tradition of democracy and the rule of law, accepted the results of the election. Fianna Fáil took power, with the support of the Labour Party.

We arrived in the market at half past six and looked over the cattle. The butchers would come up first, wanting to buy the heifers, get them weighed, and get back to open their shops at eight o'clock. Since my uncle and my cousin fed a lot of heifers, they wanted to be in good time for the butchers.

It was different for me, because I had only bullocks, which would have been sold to English buyers, or occasionally to Scots. My animals were mostly for the Manchester trade; all they were interested in was small, lean, nice beasts.

We had only a small stand, and the cattle were all our own. That meant that we were able to sell them more quickly than other standholders, who had to hold out for the minimum price that had been set by the owners.

You would stand in the market for maybe five hours and, although you had pull-ups and rubbers, it was very hard when it was wet. It's very easy nowadays. You bring them for auction to the mart, where you sit around a covered ring.

We took turns on the stand. My cousin Joe went for his breakfast first and he spent about an hour at it, down in a place in Prussia Street. I didn't care for that place, so when he came back, I went for breakfast at the City Arms Hotel.

My cousin was good at making up the accounts and getting paid, whereas I hated that part of it. I preferred going up to the weigh-scales and helping the men to sort them. These were the kind of things that my cousin didn't like.

There was always great fun between the buyers and the sellers in the market. I was lucky to have Pat Barry from Baytown beside me, because Pat was always full of the most amusing stories. Of course, a lot of them wouldn't be true, but he would always have time to tell you these stories. Pat was an extremely charitable man. He probably buried half of the poor people who worked around the market. He was a bachelor and he liked doing that sort of thing.

Jack Keogh was another man who was full of fun; he was very witty. He had a very big stand; he probably had the most cattle in the market. I remember going by his stand one day, walking some cattle down to the lower weigh-scales. I had an ash plant in my hand and was wearing an old coat, which wasn't too clean. Keogh was talking to an aristocratic-looking Englishman. Keogh called me over and said, 'Joe, how are you?'

Then he turned to the Englishman in my hearing and said, 'There's a man there who used to feed up to four hundred cattle at times. Then, ah, he just went down in the world and now he's just a drover here in the market.' The Englishman just shook his head and said, 'Ah well, these things happen.'

When I started going to the markets, the cattle were all sold by hand. You paid £20 or £25 per head and there was no such thing as selling them by weight. In order to have an idea of the weight of the beast, you had to weigh them in Mooneys, who had cattle layerages, where the Deaf and Dumb Institution is now. They charged threepence per head, or fourpence per head for weighing the cattle, so you were able to calculate however much they would be worth per hundredweight and then calculate that they were worth £22 or £23 pounds each.

After some time the system changed, so you sold them at so much per hundredweight. Then you drove up to one of the many weigh-scales around the market, where you had to queue up for them and take your turn. The buyers put a scissors-mark on their cattle as soon as they bought them, so that they could identify them when they went up on the scales.

In those days they used a bar scales, which was extremely accurate. The weigh-man asked how many cattle you had, took one glance at them over his glasses and knew that they were around ten and a half hundredweight. He would move the weight on the big brass beam to ten and a half and it would always register correctly. Then he moved the smaller weight and would calculate that the cattle were maybe seven pounds over, or under, ten and a half hundredweight. Then he rang a bell, the cattle were let out and were followed by the next lot, in a process that went on for hours.

The City Arms Hotel, where I had my breakfast, was a big building that belonged to the Conroys. I was in school with one of them, John. He ran the bars, of which there were three. The biggest bar allowed you to stand two deep at the counter. Otherwise you could go into one of three small rooms, sit down, drink, and have a conversation.

There was a second bar that opened onto Prussia Street and a third bar down in the vaults. In the vaults bar, you could either stand or sit on the barrels, and the bar man filled your glass from whichever barrel of beer you liked.

The hotel was only busy one night of the week. Nearly all of the guests were English buyers, who would stay there one night per week, for nine months of the year. The other three months of the year they'd be buying cattle in England, Scotland and Wales.

They used to leave their soiled clothes – their market clothes – in the hotel from week to week. They would share rooms with each other, maybe two to a room, or four if there were four beds in the room. There was very little furniture in the room apart from the bed. There might be a chair, otherwise you'd sit on the bed to tie on your boots. People hung their coats on nails that were driven into the back of the door.

The bigger rooms had big orange crates, which were stood on their ends. They removed the top boards, which left four posts sticking up; each man had a post on which to hang his day clothes. There were also facilities out in the passageway for washing, with soap and a brush provided.

There were two dining rooms in the City Arms Hotel. The upstairs dining room charged two shillings and sixpence for a really good breakfast, as much as you could eat. The people who were better dressed – or better educated, or something like that – usually ate in the upstairs dining room. The downstairs dining room provided breakfast for two shillings. The City Arms provided dinners and teas as well under the same arrangement. You could eat as much as you wanted, and if you wanted more you were given it without any extra charge in both rooms. The upstairs dining room had two tables. The first was a corner table which sat six people. The second was a centre table which sat twenty-six people, eleven on each side and two at the top. You might have had to wait for five or ten minutes to get a place, but nobody took very long eating their meal.

Most of the men ate steaks, with plenty of bread, butter and tea; very few of them ate onions at that hour. Others had mutton chops; I preferred rashers, eggs and black pudding for my breakfast, particularly in the cold weather of January, February and March.

Mary ran the dining room, with the help of two other girls. Most people gave her threepence or sixpence for herself. She was excellent; people were able to leave messages with her. People would come in and say, 'Did you see Mick so-and-so? Tell him I'll be above on the stand.' Or they might say, 'If Cassidy comes in, tell him I have the bales he lost.' It could be, 'Will you tell Jimmy I'm giving him them ten bullocks.' These messages were taken and delivered very quickly and carefully as soon as the man came in.

If a drunken man came in, then she escorted him down to one of the bedrooms and locked him in. If he wasn't too drunk, she'd put him sitting at the table and give him hot tea. The man or his friends would probably put a good dollop of Yorkshire Relish into the tea and would try to shake him up by giving him something to eat.

Some men had very strong views on different things and they certainly aired them at the table. There were often arguments – or even rows – between three or four men who held different shades of politics.

However, Mary would not allow the use of bad language. I'm not saying that it wouldn't occur, but the man was checked immediately for using the holy name irreverently. He'd get a very sharp check.

There was one Kildare man who regarded himself as being very grand and who fed a large number of cattle in County Kildare. I don't wish to mention his name, because his grandchildren are very well known. We weren't provided with napkins, so when he was finished his breakfast he took out his dentures and cleaned them on the tablecloth and put them back into his mouth.

There were also a number of rooms in the City Arms Hotel set aside for the banks, including the Bank of Ireland, Northern Bank and the Royal Bank. They did very big business with the lodging of cheques from the cattle market. People withdrew cash to pay for odd cattle that came in ones, twos and threes. Other people were advised at these banks.

When the cattle were sold in the market, the ropes were removed by the pen man and they were taken away by drovers and driven down to the boat at the North Wall, to go to England or Scotland.

In some cases they weren't shipped for a couple of days, because there might be no accommodation on the boat. In that case they went out to cattle parks, where they were fed and rested for their journey.

The outside cars were parked along by the cattle market. They were used by the buyers to drive the cattle down to the boat; either to see the cattle loaded or to sort them out when they got down to the boat. Sometimes they were one beast short, or one too many, and would keep the man down there until they sorted out the cattle, and then they came back again on the outside car. It was the only way really that you had, there were very few motor cars at the time.

Some of the drovers walked the cattle down to the boat with bicycles. The head drover might go three times in the day down to the boat with the cattle for certain large buyers. Then he would ride the bicycle back, because it brought him up quickly. The ones that hadn't a bicycle walked from the B&I ferry up to the Pillar on O'Connell Street and got the tram back to the cattle market.

Sheep were also sold in the market, twenty to a pen. At the end of the summer, when the lambs were being herded down to the boats, one or two of them would get underneath a tram and get entangled.

They wouldn't be bably injured but it was difficult to get them out, so the driver and the conductor had to get down on their knees and climb under the tram to pull the lamb out. The men driving the lambs had to get down under the other side of the tram and the other lambs scattered in the meantime, because they had only been taken from their mothers the night before and so they'd go looking for them.

One of the English buyers who frequented the Dublin cattle market was a man called James Heseltine. He came every week and bought cattle from my father and from myself.

Heseltine used to stay in the Four Courts Hotel. He drank quite a lot, but he was a very big heavy man and could hold a lot of drink without any sign of it showing on him. A man named Gully White used to drive an outside car for Heseltine. I imagine the reason he was called Gully was because he had a very large Adam's apple that stood out very prominently.

White used to help Heseltine up onto the outside car and they drove to Hanlon's public house, beside the cattle markets. In those days, Hanlon's had a twenty-four-hour licence for the day before the market as well as for the day of the market. Heseltine would go into Hanlon's and they'd order a bottle of champagne at six in the morning. Heseltine used to say that the champagne was great to clear your head after a night's drinking.

In order to get him over to our stall before somebody else got to him first, Jack Hynes used to go straight over to Hanlon's. Jack was a tee-totaller, so he wouldn't take any drink. As soon as Gully and James Heseltine finished their bottle of champagne, Jack Hynes walked him up the footpath, along the North Circular Road and up to our stand. By the time he came over to our stand, there wasn't the least sign of drink about him.

We had the type of cattle he liked and they killed out well for him – which meant that when the animal was processed in the abattoir, it had a high ratio of meat to wast material, such as offal, bones, etc. In fact, all of our cattle killed out well, because we had them for a good while and they were well fed off good land. He wanted big cattle, twelve-hundred-weight bullocks, and he would buy twelve-hundredweight heifers if he could get them. He had an abattoir in Bradford and the forequarters of the cattle were sold to the Jews. The hindquarters were sold – not by the pound but by the stone – to farmers who had a large number of men working for them and who had to provide one or two meals per day to their workers.

We put the cattle and the price to him, and he'd bid us for them. I don't say that we sold them straight away, but he always bid us for them and would come back afterwards and we'd give them to him, as the case may be. He was a marvellous man to make up prices for cattle on a bid;

three-eighths of a penny and five-eighths and all this sort of thing.

He was a very big man, with a tremendous tummy. When he'd be writing the cheque for the cattle, he'd rest the chequebook on top of his stomach. As he wrote he'd say, 'Joe, it's not every man who can write a cheque on his belly', which is very true of course.

He was full of fun and full of jokes. The journey from Bradford to Liverpool, followed by a boat trip to Dublin, was very tiring and tedious. It gave him plenty of time to think out his stories and the things he could do. On one occasion he was bored on the train and he got talking to a young commercial traveller, who was selling lady's underwear. He told Heseltine that it was very hard to sell the underwear, but Heseltine told him that he just needed to know how to do it. Heseltine took the sample and went from carriage to carriage along the train, selling quite an amount of lady's underwear along the train.

In his latter days he started to drink a bit too much and started keeping a bottle of whiskey in his inside pocket. As he handled the cattle, he had an adept way of loosening the cork with his left hand, taking the bottle out with his right and taking a mouthful of whiskey.

After that he mightn't be in form for writing out cheques or making up the accounts, so he'd sign a number of blank cheques and would ask my cousin Joe to go around and pay people. He'd give Joe a list of the cattle he bought on the various stands, and Joe would pay for them while Heseltine sat in the City Arms Hotel.

Heseltine was most anxious that I go over to visit him in Bradford for a week, when I was around seventeen or eighteen years old. But my father thought that he might not be a good influence on me, so I never got the opportunity to go to Bradford.

However, my parents met him on one occasion when they were in Harrogate. They often went over to Harrogate, which was a popular spa near Leeds, to take the waters. They asked James Heseltine and his wife to come along to dinner one evening.

Mother was upset, because she thought that James mightn't turn up, but to their surprise, both he and his wife showed up in evening clothes, beautifully dressed. They had a very pleasant evening and then Heseltine took my father around to various farmer's places and small markets, to show him the cattle being sold.

After he retired, he used to go every second or third day to be shaved by a certain barber in Bradford. Because he was elderly and would take the odd drink, he would fall asleep as the barber was shaving him. On one particular occasion, he came in as usual and sat down on the chair. When the barber was finished shaving him, he tipped him on the shoulder and said, 'Hey, Mister James, you may get up now, you're clean and shaven.' Heseltine didn't stir. He gave him a bit of a shake to wake him up and then he realised that he was dead, that he had died in the chair.

Heseltine only had one son, who was no use. He paid his passage to Canada, he put him on the boat, and that was the last I ever heard of the son.

Another man who bought a lot of cattle from me was Jim Metham, who came from Sayle, outside of Manchester. He only wanted small cattle; they could be as small as eight-hundredweight, and he didn't care as long as they were good meat. He didn't care for animals that were more than ten-hundredweight.

He wanted what they called the 'Manchester trade'. These were lean cattle that were used to make hotpot. Everybody in a Manchester family might be working, so they ate hotpot. They put a layer of potatoes into a cooking dish, covered it with meat, followed by a layer of vegetables, a layer of potatoes and then another layer of meat. This was cooked slowly in the range, and when the whole family arrived home at one o'clock it could be spilled out onto their plates to provide a good meal. The black Kerry cattle were particularly sought after for the Manchester trade, because they were very lean and light.

Jim Metham bought around one hundred cattle per week from March until the beginning of September. From September onwards he bought one hundred and twenty cattle per week, because the demand for beef rose. In those days, nobody ate lamb after the first of September, they changed to beef, so he bought twenty cattle extra.

When I was twenty years old, Jim Metham asked me to come over to Manchester to stay with him and his wife. Father consented, and we left on the early cattle boat, which left Dublin at around twelve o'clock. It had accommodation – of sorts – for between six and eight people. The cattle buyers sat in the small cabin and played cards, although I didn't take part.

Once we got to England, the captain took the Manchester Ship Canal to Manchester, while Metham and I took the train. The following day, we saw the cattle in the pens in the big abattoir in Manchester.

In those days, Friday was a fast day and Catholics wouldn't eat meat. I wouldn't say that the Methams had any religion. Jim used to say that he was a freemason; I suppose that he regarded that as his religion. On Thursday evening I told his wife that I didn't eat meat on Fridays, just so that she would know.

'Oh,' she said. 'I understand that, I know you don't eat meat tomorrow, I'll have something else for you.'

When I came down to my breakfast on Friday morning, a plate of rashers, eggs and black pudding was put in front of me. I put the rashers to one side with the pudding and she came along and said, 'Eh Joe, you not like your rashers?'

'I'm sorry Mrs Metham,' I said. 'I don't eat meat on a Friday.'

'That ain't meat,' she said. 'Them's bacon.'

That was just the way she looked at it.

My father and I were with the Methams in Wales on another occasion and we went to a place on a Friday. He ordered ham for us and father said, 'I'm sorry; we don't eat meat on a Friday.'

'That's ain't meat,' he said. 'That's 'am.'

That was his view on it; it wasn't ours.

The cattle going to England had to be insured, by law. If – as happened perhaps once per week – out of all the cattle travelling you had an animal with a broken leg or a broken hip, they were paid for by the insurance policy. The insurance company was run by the cattle trade.

The cattle on the boat had to be scissor-marked in a certain way, so that when the beast was taken off the boat at Birkenhead or Manchester, the insurance company would know whose animal it was. You could put in a claim for the value of your beast and if it was badly damaged, then you were paid the full value of that animal.

There were cases where men claimed more than the actual value of the beast. However, out of the hundreds of thousands of cattle that were exported, there was rarely any dispute over the value. If there was, a barrister was called in, who made a decision based on the merits of the case.

The insurance company had an enormous amount of money and only paid out less than a half of one percent of this in claims. The company had as much as £20 million just lying there. This was just in case the whole ship went down with six or seven hundred cattle, in which case the claim would be enormous. However, to my knowledge no ships sank in peacetime.

My father told me a story about a drover who used to go over every week with the cattle belonging to some Englishman. He looked after them on the boat and then he unloaded them and looked after them as they were loaded on trains for Birkenhead or Manchester.

On one particular occasion, he had been in a pub getting something to eat before he got on the boat, because he knew that he wouldn't get anything to eat on the cattle boat. It was during the summer, and as he walked along the North Wall he realised that he had left his coat in the public house. He ran back to the public house, collected his jacket and ran down to the boat, only to find that the gangway had been lifted and that the boat had started to move out. He was very disappointed because he was employed to go with the cattle and the fault was his.

The next day, he was very thankful to God that he was not on board, because this particular vessel was torpedoed off Wicklow by a German submarine. It was during the First World War and there was always the risk of being torpedoed. They used to change their course so that the submarines wouldn't see them, but all of the people on this boat were drowned. He must have said his prayers well that morning.

The Englishmen at the Dublin cattle market were very nice gentlemanly men, but a man called John Shaw was probably the most gentlemanly of the lot. I'd say he was better educated that the others at the market. He would buy bullocks from me, and his cousin Arthur would buy heifers from my uncle, all of which went to the north of England. His brother Randall would buy very large number of milking cows each week and another cousin Norman would also buy bullocks and heifers.

There were two other men who used to buy cattle from my uncle and cousins, but the only reason I mention them is because their names were unusual. The first was called Taylor Ragg, who used to tell me that he was 'only a poor boy'. He was in his mid-forties and was very thin. In those days you could buy a good new suit for fifty shillings. I would say that the value of his clothing was around ten shillings, so you can imagine that he was pretty poor-looking.

Raggs used to pay for cattle with cheques paid by a man called Horsefall. The cheques were always postdated, so that Horsefall saw the cattle in England before the cheque could be cashed over here. You took a certain risk taking those cheques, but it was very rare that anybody ever got stuck in the cattle market. It was done on a word-of-mouth basis from start to finish and was very honourably conducted on both sides.

There was a lot of etiquette in the cattle markets. For example, if a man bid you £20 for your cattle and you turned him down, and if the second and third men bid you £20, then you gave the cattle to the first man. That was just the etiquette of it.

The second man that bought from my uncle was Piggy Moss, who used to come occasionally during the summer. The other English men despised him, because they thought that he let the side down. He didn't wear a jacket or a waistcoat. He lived in a cap, with the braces of his trousers over a dirty heavy woollen over-vest. He brought his son along with him too, a queer-looking fellow. Sometimes they had a girl with them, a big blonde. That was very unusual: you hardly ever saw a woman in the market, unless they were selling fruit or something.

There were also quite a number of north-of-Ireland cattle buyers, who bought all types of cattle. Joe McGowan, who was a Catholic, came every two weeks and bought cattle for the Falls Road area of Belfast.

Simon Carson was one very nice man; he used to buy large numbers of cows. Britain McGahey and the Pryce brothers were very big in the cows. The Pryces would buy nearly a whole trainload of cows, for the shipyard workers in Belfast. The Pryces had butcher shops of their own, but they also bought for other butchers.

Of course these men were Protestants, but you got on quite well with them, except for a week before the Twelfth of July, when they were absolutely unbearable. It was hard to know what to say to them. They were cursing the Pope and they were cursing the priests, and others of them would curse the clergy of each side for stirring up trouble. The week after the Twelfth, they'd arrive down, and it was obvious that they'd been drinking heavily. I remember on one occasion that Britain McGahey had his arm in a sling and that his face was all cut. Nobody dared ask him what happened, but presumably he was in some kind of a row.

I knew one Belfast man called Clem Bell, who was approached the week before Christmas by a man who wanted him to buy cattle in Dublin.

'Look,' he said to Clem Bell. 'Bring my son along with you and buy a wagon or two of cattle with him, but keep your eye on him the whole time, because he's liable to start drinking and might miss the market.'

Bell was also a man that could drink a lot, but he looked after himself a bit better. But this young fellow – William John was his name, quite a usual name among Protestants – gave Bell the slip. On the morning of the market, there was no sign of him. Bell knew that when he went back to Belfast William John's father would be furious with him, because he couldn't buy the cattle without William John. So he thought it best to prepare the father before he arrived in Belfast. He went over to the post office beside Hanlon's and wrote out a telegram which said:

Dublin market small and dear
Willy John did not appear
Willy John is on the beer.

It was quite usual for pen-men and drovers who had made a bit of money to start dealing in cattle and sheep in a small way. It happened that one of these drovers started to buy some sheep, and he got on extremely well. He was regarded as an extremely decent young man, who was very well deserving of getting on and well deserving of credit. He was shipping the sheep and lambs to England, selling them and bringing the cash back for the following Thursday.

One of the reasons why he did so well was that people like my father and Pat Barry used to give him a week's credit. He always paid them the following week before he bought anything else from them. However, of a day he did not turn up, and father went to Pat Barry and asked him had he seen so-and-so. Pat Barry hadn't seen him either and they wondered whether he was sick.

When he didn't show up the following week, the various people who had given him credit were extremely disappointed that he had done such a thing to them. The amount of money would have been small in each case, but they felt that they had been let down badly by such a decent young man.

They heard nothing from him for a couple of years, until one morning my father got a letter from him, which had been posted in England. He said that he wanted to meet my father in the Gresham Hotel at ten o'clock on a particular market morning.

My father wondered whether it was genuine, but he showed up, as did Pat Barry and as many as twenty other men. They all wondered whether the man would show up. They were shown into a special room and at ten o'clock the man walked into the room.

He said, 'Gentlemen, I want to apologise for what I have done, I was stuck. However, I have done very well in the meanwhile, thanks to you men who helped me. As I said in my letter, you should have brought your accounts with you and I will give you 3 percent interest on the money I got from you.'

Three percent was a very good interest rate at that time. Each of them presented their accounts with the 3 percent interest and they were paid by a cheque that was drawn on an Irish bank.

After each of them had been paid, he said, 'I want to thank you all for being so good to me. I have prospered, I have done well in England, I am leaving on the twelve o'clock boat from the North Wall, and none of you will ever see me again.'

So that was that, and none of them ever heard from him again.

12

JOE'S FAIR DAYS

There are men my age and older, and not much younger, who miss the fairs very much. You'd find a great sense of comradeship at the fairs. We helped each other and we had any amount of fun among ourselves, telling stories. Many of them were made up, so you'd have two or three fellows making up a good story. One would tell the story and the others would verify it for the man that it was being told to. They'd say it would be absolutely true.

The first fair I went to without my father was Baltinglass fair in March, while I was still in Clongowes. I drove with Mattie Ward and bought five grand bullocks. I remember them very well. I brought them home and my father looked at them and said, 'Where are the other five?'

'What other five,' I asked.

'Well,' he said. 'If you were able to buy five really good cheap bullocks like those, then you must have been able to give five more anyway.'

That's all he said, but it was a compliment.

I started attending fairs alone in the late 1920s, when I was around seventeen or eighteen years old. My father sent me to Westport to buy some cattle, saying that I wouldn't be able to make much of a mistake there, because the cattle were all small and the money would be very low.

I went to Westport and bought a number of cattle. Towards the end of the day I wanted to buy one beast or two cows to fill up the wagon. I saw a lovely-looking bullock, of the highland type, which were known as 'kyloes' at that time. The local cows had been crossed with an imported bull to give them a bit of size, by a doctor from near Mulranny.

This particular animal belonged to Martin Moran – who farmed with his brother Michael – and was standing along a wall in Westport. I spoke to the man who was selling him, and we weren't five minutes making the deal, because he didn't charge me too much. I told him that I wanted him brought up to the railway at once, and I put a scissors mark on him, to indicate that I had bought him and that he was now my property.

The minute I turned him around, I noticed that he had a huge lump on the side of his face, which you couldn't see when he was standing along the wall. I protested to Martin Moran.

'Sure, what harm is on him,' he said. 'He wouldn't put on that condition if there was anything wrong with him, sure.'

I asked him what happened to the beast.

'To be perfectly honest with you, that bullock was fed with a lot of others on the mountains near Mulranny,' he said. 'It's six months since I saw him, so I couldn't tell you more than that. But it doesn't seem to have done him any harm.'

I was very pleased with the beast, but I got a certain amount of ragging from the other farmers and cattle men, who said that I had got caught out by Moran.

As we were going back on the train that evening, they asked what my father would say when he found out, and all that sort of thing. The bullock was shipped home immediately, but I went on to the Ballinrobe fair that afternoon, so I wasn't able to tell my father anything about him. He saw the animal the following morning and told my mother, who told him not to be too hard on me, that I was young and could make a mistake.

When the beast arrived at Gunnocks, they painted the lump with a very strong tincture of iodine, and the lump disappeared altogether. My father and I sent this lovely bullock to the Christmas fat stock show in Dublin. A great number of people looked at him on account of the size of his horns and his golden hair down to the ground. He didn't get any prize, but he was certainly a curiosity and he paid very well.

It may be of interest to note that each of us, when we bought cattle, put a scissors-mark on them. That means that we cut the animal's hair with a scissors. I put a big 'W' on mine; other people put three cuts; Laurence of Fieldstown put an arrowhead; my cousins put a cross. We all knew each other's scissors-mark, so if somebody's beast got lost we were able to say, 'Ah look, your bullock is above with Delaney's cattle at the station, we saw the big "X" on him.' The marks remained on the animals for some time until their hair grew back.

After the war, when the Dutch came to buy cattle, a man called Wezenfeld marked them all with roman numerals. It was extremely interesting to all of the market people to see the wondrously quick way it was done. He had a man with him, of course. It was extraordinary to see these roman numerals that were absolutely beautifully done. Sometimes you'd see 1,100 or 1,200 cattle with roman numerals on them. The man marked them down in a notebook, noting that Joseph Ward's cattle were, for example, the cattle with numbers between ten and eighteen. If a beast didn't kill out well, or if there was any problem with it, he'd tell you that the animal had been damaged. He wouldn't be expecting money back or anything like that, but he always knew that the animal belonged to Joseph Ward and not to Joe Soap.

In those days, a lot of the hotels, lodging houses and 'ating houses were terribly bad. There were no tourists around and anyway, they weren't going to stay in places like Balla and Ballinrobe. They'd stay in decent places like Mularanny, Claremorris or Westport. Once cars came, you could stop in decent hotels and drive over in the morning.

In Ballinrobe you could either stay in Stanners Hotel or in the Railway Hotel. I've stayed in other places that I don't want to mention the name of – they've been done up since – that were full of rats and were disgusting.

The Railway Hotel wasn't too bad. It had a huge dining room and a huge mahogany table the length of the room, but no food, no plates, no knives of any kind.

On one occasion I stayed in Stanners Hotel, which was a bit outside the place. My father had taught me a number of things about staying in these places. One thing was to jam something against the door to stop people coming in during the night. There would be fellows arriving in drunk off a late train and he wouldn't care. He'd just peg himself onto the bed and that was that. But I remember one night, the door was very dunny altogether and I had to wedge the chair against the handle of the door. I never slept well in these places and sure enough, at around half past one in the morning, there was a rat-tat-tat and hammering and all of the rest of it. The next thing one of the panels broke and I saw Ned West looking in at me with his hard hat on him, muttering 'I'm sorry I woke you up, I'm sorry I woke you up' and away he went.

Many of the places you had to stop in those days were extremely bad, in terms of the beds and the whole outfit of the place. You tried one bed and then you tried another to see if there would be any bed that might be dry and comfortable.

Gort was noted for being bad. They had only one big fair every year and there was practically no accommodation of any kind. The first time I went to it a man asked me had I any place booked, so I told him that I had written to so-and-so.

'You needn't mind that,' said he. 'If a fellow gets down before you, he'll get into the bed and they'll keep no check on you. The best thing for you to do is to go to the Garda barracks. They know places where they'd be able to put you up for the night.'

I'm glad to say that I never had to go to the Garda barracks.

A Dublin cattle dealer told me that he arrived in a town in the west of Ireland at eleven o'clock at night. When he arrived at the house the woman said that she hadn't known he was coming, that he had said that he wouldn't be going to this particular fair.

'Ah well, I got word last night that I was to get some cattle down here. Can you fix me up?'

'I'll manage all right,' she said.

She brought him down to a room and opened the door. Her daughter, a girl of around eleven years, was in bed and she shook her up and said, 'Get up out of that.' The girl pulled herself together and stumbled along. It was a cold March night and he was very glad that she had the bed heated up.

I remember staying in one place in Gort on 16 March. The weather was cold and awful and we were eating in the dining room, which had a table and chairs and no carpet on the floor. There was a large broken pane of glass in the window, looking out onto the street.

We were sitting around the tables, with our hats and coats on, trying to keep warm. The men who smoked pipes were in the habit of spitting into the fire, but there was no fire. There was a one-bar electric fire and so they spat on the bar of the electric fire, which sounded like something frying. It didn't help the heat either.

151

One of the Donnellys from Kilmessan was persuaded to take off his hat and to shove it into the broken window. It kept out some of the cold until we managed to get our tea.

I was anxious to get off to bed, but the man who ran the place was anxious that we all drink whiskey. Of course, we'd have to pay for it. I wasn't a whiskey-drinking man, or any kind of a drinking man, but he wasn't inclined to let me go.

Finally he handed me a candle in a bottle and told me that there was a bed for me at the end of the garden. I couldn't see what the place was like, but I got into it anyway and it had to do for the night.

A small thing that used to intrigue both my father and myself was how quickly the uneducated dealer, or tangler, could go to sleep. If you were in a room with them, they came in, looked at you and said, 'That's a fine night' or 'That's a wet night'. Then they went over to the bed, threw their overcoat on it and hung their hat on the end of it. They sat on the bed and threw off their big heavy boots, which always made a terrible bang on the wooden boards because there were no carpets. Finally they threw themselves into the bed, and in less than the time you'd say 'go to sleep', the man was fast asleep.

My father and I thought that better-educated people would take a while before they'd fall asleep. I often marvelled at it, how quickly they would go to sleep with their clothes on; there was nothing on their mind to worry them at all.

I wouldn't get up before daylight to buy anything. A lot of people, particularly the northerners, would carry flash lamps with them, but I wouldn't buy cattle until it was bright, because you could be stuck with a lame one or a blind one.

When I wouldn't get up, some of the dealers and tanglers would think that I was sleepy or lazy. On a couple of occasions they pulled the bed-clothes off me and pulled me out onto the floor.

'Look,' I'd say. 'I'm not getting up for another hour until there's light.'

'Ah,' they'd start saying, 'that's bad luck.' Then they'd bang the door and go out.

I remember one occasion in the big Railway Hotel in Galway. The 'Boots', one of the male employees, came up one morning, rushed into the room and said, 'I've called you a couple of times already. He said you must have fallen asleep.'

Of course I heard the banging on the door, but I wasn't going to get up, because I knew that I didn't need to get up for another hour or more. He had evidently gotten into trouble for not calling people on previous occasions. On this occasion he came into the room, pulled the bedclothes off me, caught me by the arm and pulled me out onto the floor.

'Look,' I said, 'I'm not getting up.'

Says he, 'Are you not one of the pig dalers?'

'No,' I said. 'I am not a pig dealer.'

'Ah,' he said. 'I'm sorry. I thought you were a pig daler and they all wanted to be called at half-four.'

'You should have asked me beforehand,' I said. I needn't tell you that I wasn't able to go back to sleep.

Often when I went to get my lunch, you'd have fifteen or sixteen country men sitting at a table that was made for twelve. They'd be eating over your shoulder, it was pretty awful.

On one occasion I was given a piece of blue meat; it was awful looking. I never saw anything like it. You got a few potatoes and a bit of cabbage and more often a bit of turnip. Ah, I said, I might get a decent bit to eat on the train, so I pushed the blue meat to one side and ate whatever else was there. I went to pay the bill for my bed and said to the girl, what do I owe you?

'Oh, Mr Ward,' said the girl. 'We're not charging you anything.'

'Why?' said I.

'Oh,' she said. 'You were given the wrong dinner, you were given the dinner that was for the country men. We had the meat for you separate and the maid didn't know and gave you the meat, so we're not charging you anything.'

'Well,' I said. 'I never saw blue meat before.'

Loughrea Fair was always held on a Friday during Lent. In those days you could not eat meat on a Friday, and I don't care for eggs. It was a case of bread and tea with nothing else. I bought a tin of sardines in a shop in the town and brought it into Mrs Moylan's, where I was staying. I said to her, will you open up that tin of sardines and bring them upstairs to the sitting room with tea and bread and butter. She asked me whether I wanted it straight away, and I said that I would have a shave first and I'd let her know when I was ready.

She thought that she would give me a nice warm meal, rather than having cold sardines in March. I went down after a short while and found that she had boiled the sardines and mixed them with boiled turnips. A plate of mush and mess arrived up to me and I was absolutely disgusted with the thing.

Well, I wasn't caught out that way again. The next time, I opened my own box of sardines and ate them along with the tea and bread and butter.

Another time I was staying in Miss Stafford's in Longford town. She kept mostly northerners, but you got a small room to yourself and the place itself was very clean.

Most people would arrive in at the same time for breakfast, and they were all very hungry. They were also very anxious to get finished, so that they could pay the men for the cattle they'd bought and get away out of the town as quickly as possible, to get home. They didn't like to be held up by any delay at breakfast.

Miss Stafford was used to keeping two or three bank clerks, who came in at regular hours, and she would do the catering herself. For the fair, she took in an untrained girl for the day, who knew very little about anything.

On this particular occasion we were all at a long table and the delay was endless. Most of the people at the table were northerners, and they were all shouting, 'Where's my breakfast?', 'Bring in my breakfast', 'Where have you the butter?', 'Where's the tae?' and this sort of thing. I suppose that there was nothing ready in the kitchen and Miss Stafford – in order to buoy up the girl – told her to take a vase of flowers and put it on the table.

Well, that was the last straw. The girl turned to go back to the kitchen and a northerner grabbed the vase of flowers, which was full of water, and pegged them at the girl, hitting her on the back.

'A lot of good them is to a hungry man,' he said.

We did get fed in the end.

I remember being in the big fair of Balla, County Mayo, which was on 19 March. There would be five or six thousand cattle in the streets, packed as tight as could be. It was a killer pushing through them. I came out of the hotel in the morning and met a white bullock with spots on him, he was a grand bullock. I wasn't long making a deal with the man. I normally put a big scissors mark on the beast's right plate as soon as I bought it, but my hands were numb because of the weather. It wouldn't have been the done thing for a man in the cattle trade to wear gloves.

The crush of the cattle coming into the town meant that the cattle at the fair were bound to move a certain amount over the course of the morning. A seller might stand outside a particular shop or a particular door with his cattle, but because of the pressure, he might move a few yards, it made it very hard to find your cattle, because you might have had two or three hundred cattle in one block. It was particularly hard to find cattle in a place like Balla, where nearly all of the cattle were black.

When Paddy Hogan came in as Minister for Agriculture in the early 1920s, he was regarded as the best minister for agriculture in Europe. He was certainly very good; there is no doubt about that. But I think he made a mistake in introducing a lot of white bulls into Connemara. His idea was to get blue-grey calves and to breed the black cattle bigger. Well, the first cross was alright, but with the second cross, all of the calves came out white and that was no help to the people down there. But that's all in the past; they're all Charolais and Herefords now.

On this particular occasion, there was a terrific shower of snow around half an hour after I bought the bullock, which meant that when I came back I was unable to find the white bullock with the blue spots. I asked everyone and I searched and searched. I started rubbing snow off the backs of the white cattle to see if I could find the bullock with the blue spots. In a place like Balla, none of the sellers would have been selling any more than four cattle. I must have been two hours looking for the beast, with people saying, 'What are you rubbing my bullock for?' and 'What do you want?' or 'He's sould!' and all that kind of thing. I always found them very disagreeable in Balla, they wouldn't give you any help. I possibly think they had very bad landlords, and people like me wouldn't be liked around there. Anyway, I never like the Balla people. But eventually I found my bullock and that was that.

There were quite a lot of women – widows, usually – selling cattle in Galway town. I never saw it anywhere else. They'd have one, two or maybe three cattle for sale. They'd be saying the rosary the whole time that they'd be waiting for a buyer to come along. If you wanted to slap their hands, to give £13 for the cattle, they'd have to change the rosary beads over to the other hand, while they held out their right hand to get the clap on it. The women were often terribly hard to deal with – impossible – I usen't to bother with them at all.

When I was just a boy, I bought a very old cow from a woman in Ballinrobe, County Mayo.. We wanted milk for the house, and my father said that since I wasn't able to milk I should get a quiet cow. This woman had a very quiet old black pollie cow; she called her Mary. I don't know what age this cow was – she could have been thirteen or fourteen years old – but I paid £6 for her.

I invited the old woman to come up to the railway, where we would load the cow with our bullocks. Because she was a cow, I knew that she'd be easier to load than the bullocks, because she'd be more used to going through a door of a house.

Anybody who has any experience of cattle or dogs will notice that they usually smell the door, or the board by the door, before they go inside. It gives them an indication as to whether the place is safe to enter.

In this case, the old cow spent a minute or two smelling the board going into the wagon and the door inside, looking around to see if everything was all right.

A big lump of a country fellow carrying an ash plant flew out and hit her a woeful wallop across the back, to make her go in, thinking that she wasn't going fast enough. So, by dad, the woman had an ash plant too and she threw it out and hit the man an equally good belt across the shoulders, saying to him, 'Mary knows her condition, what you don't.'

Looking over my father's old account books and my fair books, you'll see regular entries saying 'Custom, £1.20', or '£1.40', or something like that. I will now explain the custom system.

The best example is the fair green in Ballinasloe, which – along with the rest of the town – was the property of Lord Clancarty. He charged sixpence per head for each beast – bullock, heifer, cow or bull – as they left the fair green. He charged twopence for sheep and a shilling for a horse.

In theory, the charges were for the upkeep of the green, but not one penny was spent on the fair green, which was always a muddy bog. He probably put it in his own pocket, or it may have contributed towards improvements in the town.

They put up huts on the outskirts of the town, in which the customs man sat, sheltering from the weather. You paid your sixpence per head, so that you'd be allowed to take them home, or up to the railway.

You'd be walking behind five or six lots of cattle and, as you approached the customs gap, you'd be stopped by half a dozen men with sticks. These men were employed by Clancarty, and they'd say, 'Who owns them cattle?'

The man who had bought them shouted out, 'They're mine.'

'How many have you?'

'Sixty-two.'

They were counted as they passed the customs gap, and when you got to the hut the customs man told you how much you owed. You paid him, and that was that.

Sometimes the owner was not with the cattle. Chancing his arm, he might have told the seller to bring the cattle up to the railway and to give them to Jack Reynolds to load them. The seller would often agree to pay the custom and to collect the amount from the buyer when he returned to the fair.

However, sometimes the seller arrived at the customs gap without knowing the name of the buyer.

'Ah,' he'd say, 'he's a Dublin man.'

They'd ask him who, and he wouldn't know.

'Are you going to pay the custom?' they'd ask.

'No, I'm not,' he'd say. 'He's going to pay it when he comes up.'

The customs men wouldn't agree to that, so the cattle were turned out into a paddock until the buyer came to get them out. The trouble with that is there might be a hundred or more cattle in the field and you had to sort your own cattle out of them. It was just one field of mud, as though it had been ploughed, except that there would be water lying in parts of it. It never happened to me, because I had the experience of my father and my uncle, so I knew the ropes well. But I saw it happen to other people and it could be terribly annoying.

In some cases the customs clerk might be collecting for Lord Clancarty himself, who would have had the rights to collect tolls from an old charter, going back to 1600 or 1700. If the custom was being collected on behalf of Clancarty, or some other landlord, the customs man would often round down an uneven number: a pound and eightpence was charged as a pound. He might also put a cap on the amount he charged, if you had a large number of cattle or if you were a constant visitor to the fair.

Some landlords, rather than going to the bother of employing men for the twelve fairs of the year, auctioned the custom. A shopkeeper in the town would bid the highest amount for it, hoping to make the money back and make a decent profit on top of that. These men were often present in the customs huts to make sure that everybody paid up the full amount.

In some places they didn't charge anything, but in other places they did. In Loughrea the money went to the town council as rates payments, to pay the expense of running the town.

At other fairs – such as Carlow – it was the sellers who had to pay the custom, before they were allowed into the fair. There were two entrances into the magnificent ring in Carlow, which made it really easy to collect the tolls. Carlow was like a park, with trees all through it, a weigh-scale, a canteen, and pens for the cattle.

In those days the seller usually gave the buyer a luck penny of two shillings and sixpence. In Carlow, the man would say to you, 'I'm giving you two bob, because I paid sixpence custom on the beasts.' I was quite happy with that arrangement.

The most unpleasant experience that I ever had at a fair took place in Galway. It was the September fair in Galway, when the cattle were brought in from the Aran Islands. This was during the 1930s, during the Economic War, when cattle were worth practically nothing.

The Aran Island cattle used to come in for the September fair, they had to swim behind the islanders' boats. They used to consume a certain amount of salt water and it was better to let them empty out before you showed them at the fair. As well as that, the hair came up better on them when they dried out. The cattle couldn't swim back to the islands, so if they didn't sell the cattle they'd have to rent land to keep them until the next fair.

The King of the Aran Islands was a man called Pat Mullen. His daughter acted in a picture called *Man of Aran*. Mullen came to me and said that he had five bullocks standing down at the statue.

'I want to sell them and I'm getting £5 a piece for them,' he sasid. 'I won't sell them for £5, but I'll sell them for £5 5 shillings, or for five guineas.'

I looked at the bullocks from a distance and I saw that there was a local man called Kyne buying them.

'Look,' I said to Mullen. 'I can't go in on those cattle because Kyne is buying them.'

'Oh,' he says. 'Kyne is not buying them, he's just standing over there, he's been there for the past two or three hours. He knows that I can't bring them back to the island, so he wants to wear me down with them.'

I'd buy eighteen or twenty-seven cattle at most fairs, at that time I used to feed between four and five hundred cattle in the year. I used to keep them for at least six months, on around a hundred acres of land over at Kilcreagh, which belonged to my father's aunt, who was a Miss Cuffe.

He told me that he'd bring them up to the railway station and put them into a wagon and would tell the railway people to put my other cattle with them afterwards. I agreed to do that, even though I refused to go near the cattle.

However, Kyne found out that I had bought the cattle. I had never seen a person in such a bad state; he was frothing at the mouth and beating the ground with his ash plant, looking for the man who bought the cattle behind his back. He said that he'd split me in two.

My cousin happened to be there. He came to me and said that Kyne was absolutely in the horrors and that he would get the guards to protect me. A guard came along to protect me until I had finished loading the cattle and paying the men.

There was one train porter by the name of Dick Gannon, who used to travel to nearly all of the fairs in the west. He had been a policeman before he joined the railway company.

Dick was always very fond of me, and when Kyne came up to take the cattle out of the wagon, Dick wouldn't let him. Once the cattle were booked into the wagon, they were the property of the railway company, so he refused to allow Kyne to unload them.

I went back to the hotel after loading the cattle and was able to get out to the train through the back door of the hotel.

The incident shook me up, because the man would have liked to have split me in two. Several local people – such as the Glynns from the Loughrea and Gort area – told me that he was absolutely dangerous when he was in the horrors.

Another time I was at the fair in Gort, which started at around three o'clock in the morning. I was out in the street walking up and down and was fed up with not buying anything, so I bought a big bullock with the money in it. I gave four pounds for him, but he was a huge beast.

Later in the day, when I tried to move him out, I discovered that he had a club foot. He could walk all right, but I decided to 'throw him up', as the expression goes. But a few fellows with big ash plants came around and they started showing me the ash plants. So – I hardly need tell you – I said, 'All right, I'll take him up to the railway station', and there was no more about it. They could be very rough at that time, particularly in the south of Ireland.

On another occasion I was coming from Athenry fair and got into a carriage with a large number of dairy men. One of them was a man named Joe Doherty, who had been drinking poitín heavily during the morning and during the day. He didn't really know what he was doing, but he took exception to my being in the carriage.

It was an old-fashioned single carriage, which had no corridor. After a short while I moved to another part of the train, where there was a corridor, and took a seat.

Doherty wasn't in his right mind, and he followed me up the train. When he found me in another carriage, with a lady and a gentleman, he went for me and opened the window.

'I'll peg you out onto the railway line,' he said.

The lady and gentleman were so frightened that they left the carriage at once. The other men suspected that Doherty had gone after me and came looking for us.

One of them was a very powerful Roscommon man called Pat

'Flat-footed' Burke. He was a professional loader, who knew how to make sure that the cattle kept their heads up and their legs down as they were being loaded onto the wagons. At that time the cattle had horns, and if they dropped their heads they could be dragged down by another animal's legs and get walked on. I had often employed him to load cattle, giving him half a crown per wagon, to beat the cattle into the wagon.

Burke grabbed Doherty and threw him down on the seat. Then he sat on his chest to keep him secure, as I went to another carriage. Doherty was then brought down to the dining car and one of the attendants locked him into it for some time, before he broke the door and got out. Fortunately, by that time, we had already reached Broadstone Station in Dublin.

I told my father about the incident when I met him at Broadstone station and suggested that we get the Guards. My father said that it would be better not to, with which I agreed.

Doherty was terribly ashamed of that incident. I met him a number of times and he always kept his eyes down on the ground when he was passing me.

A number of years later, I had ten big, ugly, short-horn heifers at the Dublin market. He wanted that kind of heifer, but he didn't dare come near me. He sent another man to bid me for them. The other man told me that they were for Joe Doherty, but that on account of the row he didn't want to come near me.

'He said to give you all they were worth,' he said. To give him his due, Doherty gave me a good price for them and I gave him a decent luck penny and we were good friends after that.

Pat 'Flat-footed' Burke used to load cattle together with two brothers from Roscommon, the Reynolds brothers. One of the brothers, Jack Reynolds, had only one eye and he covered the bad eye with his cap.

The arrangement was, if you hadn't paid them when they were loading the wagons, then they collected their money from you in the carriage, before the train left the station.

Because Jack Reynolds had only one eye, he had to scrutinise all of the people in carriage, to see which ones owed him money. In other words, one eye travelled down one side of the carriage and then up the other side, looking at all of the people.

There was one particular gentleman from County Galway, I'll call him Doyle. He was very elderly when he got married, but he married an elderly widow with a great deal of money. He lived near Phibsborough church in Dublin, which was convenient for going to mass. He had a remarkable blue frieze coat, which went from his collar down to his feet. Everybody said 'Doyle and his oul' blue coat', because he wore it everywhere. I'm sure that it was a very old coat, but it was a great coat to keep out the rain and the wet. On account of getting a lot of money with the widow, he though a lot of himself and he travelled first-class with people who were a different type to him.

Jack Reynolds came along looking for his luck pennies one day, as the train was standing in one of the stations. He looked around the carriage and said to each of the persons, 'Ah, that's a fine evening Mr So-and-so' or 'Ah, that's a grand evening Mr Such-and-Such', and would usually prefix 'mister' to most of the people. But of course, knowing Doyle and who he was and his origins, he just said 'Good evening 'Doyle'.

When he closed the carriage, Doyle was very annoyed and said out loud, 'Huh, that fella with the one eye, saying to me, good evening Doyle, speaking to me like that, a man of my manes.'

Of course, any means that he had, they came from his wife.

Paying for cattle and getting back a luck penny was always a nuisance. I have often seen country men search in all their pockets to find coins. If it's a wet day they could have two coats on them and a jacket. They find a couple of coins in one and they find one in another. They do their trousers and then they come back to the others. It can be endless if you're trying to get a luck penny out of them.

The luck penny was a decided advantage, because it covered a great deal of your expenses. It paid your hotel expenses and a good portion of your train fair. In the modern mart, you don't have any luck penny of any kind; you just get paid the selling price. You also don't get paid on the spot, it might be three or four days, even over a week, before you get paid. It's the same with meat factories. Whereas with both the fairs and the old market you got paid on the spot, which was a great advantage.

On another occasion, I bought two bullocks in Balla, from a nice old man named McGowan. The typical payment arrangement in Balla was that you'd agree to meet in Macklin's Hotel or in Valkenberg's Hotel. It's hard to say whether Macklin's or Valkenberg's was the worst hotel, but either way you'd end up sharing your room with somebody else. Fortunately the train used to leave at three o'clock in the afternoon, so you were more than pleased to get into the comfort of the train to bring you home.

The station in Balla was around a mile from the town and Macklin's Hotel was at the other end of the town. I liked to leave at two o'clock, to give me plenty of time to walk up to the station with my bags and my coat. To my annoyance, McGowan did not turn up to get paid for his cattle. On principle, I always liked to pay for the cattle on the day. If you didn't pay them on the day and if they didn't write to you for payment, then you might have to go back to the next fair to pay them, even if you weren't interested in going to that fair on the following occasion.

I was dressed and ready to go, with my soiled clothes packed in the bag. As I was about to give up and go to the station, I saw him in the hall of the hotel, which was packed with other buyers, sellers and countrymen. I went down to him and told him that I had been waiting for him.

He looked surprised and said, 'You're not the man that bought my two bullocks.'

'Oh yes, I am.'

'Oh no, you're not.'

'I am the man that bought your two bullocks', but he said that I wasn't.

'Whether you think I did or you think I didn't, I'm going to pay you for them.'

'Well now,' he said, 'you're a very decent young man to offer to pay for me two cattle, but I wouldn't accept the money from you.'

I asked him what the buyer of his cattle was like.

'Well,' he said, 'he had a bright coat on him, a white coat on him.'

Most of the buyers wore light waterproof coats and the country people called them 'bright coats' or 'white coats'. They wore dark frieze coats themselves.

So I had to go upstairs again to change into my dirty clothes, my dirty coat and my dirty hat. Then I walked down the stairs into the hall to McGowan.

'Ah, there you are,' said McGowan when he saw me. 'I was waiting here, for you to come and pay me for me two bullocks.'

The banking system was different altogether in those days. In the 1930s, you went to the manager in the branch where you had your account and you said to him, 'I want you to advise the Athenry branch for £1,000 on the twenty-third of the month.'

Since you'd given him due notice, he would write a letter to the manager in Athenry, if there was a bank in the town. If there wasn't, then it had to come out from Galway, Tuam or Ballinasloe. When you bought your cattle, you went to the bank and told them that there should be an advice there for you; they checked this and gave you the money.

Some of these banks were only temporary. The banks rented a very bad old thatched cottage for the day. The one in Athenry was the worst bank I've ever seen, but I'm sure that there were a few worse in the country. One half of the cottage was reasonably waterproof, but the other part had fallen in.

You entered it from the street through the kitchen door. They had a wooden plank on two stays to act as a counter. The clerks behind the counter kept the money in big orange boxes. One box had pound notes, one had five-pound notes, another had ten-pound notes, and the silver was kept in a sack. You'd tell them that you wanted so many pound notes, so many fives, and so many tens, and they'd hand them to you from the orange crates. In those days there was never any danger that anybody was going to break in and rob them.

Loughrea was the worst, from the point of view of troublesomeness. There were an enormous number of men at the fair, but there was only one bank. By the time I got down to the bank, all of the money would have been given out.

The clerks would tell me to come back at three o'clock, at which point all of the money that had been paid out would come back again, as the men who had sold their cattle would be lodging it in their accounts. The problem was that the train left at a quarter past three and you wanted to pay everybody and get out of the place.

In that case you had to write cheques, which was an awful nuisance. I remember having to write up to eighteen cheques. There would be no proper place to write them; you couldn't write them in the bank, because it was packed to suffocation. A lot of them couldn't spell out their names, and they'd say, 'Spell it any way you like yourself.' Having to write cheques was a persecution from start to finish.

You'd ask people whether they wanted to stop a luck penny off the cheque, but they'd say that it would be bad luck to stop it off a cheque, that they'd give you the luck penny out of their pocket. On a wet day they might have two or three coats on them and by the time they'd have found the few shillings and taken the cigarette packages and various items out of their pockets, the whole process was endless.

It was also dreadfully unfair to the clerks. Once the cashier went into his box at ten in the morning, he didn't get out of it. Somebody brought him a cup of tea and a sandwich, which he ate while he was paying out money. He had to stay in there from ten in the morning until three in the afternoon without any kind of a break. It was really no wonder that the bank officials kicked up over conditions like that.

Most of the people who travelled to the fairs were Catholics, and I'd say that most of us were good Catholics. Many would say the rosary each night in the chapel before the fair, and some went to mass the next day.

John Waldron was an exception. He was a very militant Protestant – he was a bit odd in ways – but he was very well liked by the Catholics. He was certainly one of the most decent men you ever met. He was a huge man and was powerfully strong. One day my father had an attack of lumbago as he was trying to carry his bag up to the hotel in Carlow, which is a long way from the station. He met John Waldron, who carried the bag up to the hotel, along with his own, even though he was as old as my father.

I remember on one occasion there was an old screw of a cow, which fell and wasn't able to get up. It was lying across what was known as 'the alleyway' and was blocking people, so Jack Waldron went over, put his arms around behind her legs, jacked her over and put her alongside the pen.

I remember that he would embarrass other Protestants – members of the Church of Ireland – by getting onto them about their religion. I attended a fair in Baltinglass, County Wicklow, which is a very Protestant area. I'd stay that half of the people selling cattle in the town were Protestant, of some denomination or other.

There was only one bank in the town at the time, which would be packed to suffocation with people trying to get money in and get money out. In those days, there were no such things as robberies or anything like that, but if there had been, they'd get plenty of money on a market day.

One day I went into the bank, and Waldron – who was a huge man – was standing in the crowd, berating another Protestant man who wouldn't give him a decent luck penny. He'd say to the man, 'Aren't you a Protestant', and the man would say shush, and Waldon would say, 'What are you shushing me for, are you ashamed of being a Protestant?', and the man would say, 'No, no, no', and he'd say, 'Well, shout out that you're a Protestant and don't be ashamed of it. Why should we be ashamed of it, the other crowd here are not ashamed to be Catholic. Give me a decent luck penny here.'

So Waldron persuaded him to hand over a decent luck penny, to get away from the embarrassment, to escape being made little of, because he wouldn't admit out loud that he was a Protestant.

On one occasion Waldon was going down to Enniscorthy on the train, reading a copy of the *Irish Times*. When he came to the end of the death notices, he said, 'Ah, my goodness, twenty-three Protestants dead, isn't that shocking.'

A man in the carriage – who had nothing to do with the cattle trade – chuckled when he heard him say this.

Waldron turned on him.

'Ha – so you're pleased that there are twenty-three of us dead?'

'Oh no,' said the man, 'not at all.'

'So what did you chuckle for?'

'Oh,' he said, 'it was just the way you said it.'

'Ah,' said Waldron to him, 'I know your type: you're just the type that would like to see all of the Protestants of the country dead.'

Oh course the man protested, but Waldron wiped the floor with him before he was finished with him.

I started travelling to fairs in a motor car in 1927, shortly after I left school. I travelled with Mattie Ward, who helped with the collecting and loading of the cattle. Mattie was always very helpful, terribly good-humoured and absolutely full of fun; he and I were really great friends.

Mattie was the yard boy at the Gunnocks when I was a young boy and he also used to look after the garden. Mattie was one of the Wards of Ruan – the 'gully' Wards – who were the oldest family of Wards in the area but were not related to us. His wife had been my nurse and they lived in a thatched cottage at Bracetown, which has since been replaced by Coakley's industrial warehouses. He kept the place extremely well. It was a lovely little place, the house, the thatch, and the garden with the roses.

In the 1890s, fewer than one thousand cottages were built annually in rural Ireland, despite the passage of the first Irish Labourers Act in 1883, the goal of which was to provide for better housing for rural workers.

At that time, labourers depended upon their employers for housing, which meant that they were completely dependent upon their employer not just for wages but also for housing and security. The only other option was to get a cottage from the county council under the restrictive terms of the 1883 legislation.

In 1894, D. D. Sheehan and J. J. O'Shee formed the Irish Land and Labour Association. Sheehan's family had been evicted in 1880, during the Land League's 'No Rent' manifesto, when his father's farm was taken over by a 'land-grabber', who paid their rent arrears. The objectives of the ILLA were to achieve tenant land purchase for tenant farmers, as well as new and improved housing, better working conditions and land for rural labourers.

The ILLA was opposed by mainstream nationalists lead by John Dillon, who rejected economic development in advance of national development, whether it was Plunkett's agricultural co-operatives, William O'Brien's tenant land purchase, or Sheehan's housing of rural labourers. Sheehan ran against an IPP candidate in Cork in 1901 and was elected to Westminster, a seat he held until 1918.

The introduction of local elections in 1898 created a political opportunity for labourers, whose votes were sought by candidates for the new county councils. This increased the political pressure for a rural housing scheme.

The Labourers Acts of 1906 provided extensive state funding for county council-erected labourer-owned cottages. This transformed the living conditions of rural labourers. Over the next five years, more than 40,000 labourers' dwellings were built in the countryside. Farmers were required to surrender an acre to each labourer, so that they could grow food for themselves, to supplement their wages.

By 1921, up to a quarter of a million people were housed under the Labourers Act, which, because of better housing, led to a decline in tuberculosis, typhoid and scarlet fever in rural areas.

After the First World War, the ILLA amalgamated with the Irish Transport and General Workers Union (ITGWU), which was the strongest union in the Irish

labour movement. The influence of the labourers could be seen in the strength of the
Irish Labour Party, which became the leading opposition party in Dáil Eireann after
the War of Independence.

Mattie Ward was the first man to drive the Essex motor car we got in 1926. I was in Clongowes at the time, and they thought it would be a good idea to get a car so that they could drive the thirteen miles to visit me. We were allowed one visit per month, on a Sunday.

My father, Mattie and I used to go to Blessington fair to buy cattle. Mattie would sleep in the back of the car until we had bought cattle. We wouldn't buy many – ten at the most – which Mattie would drive home on foot. He liked to be leaving Blessington at eleven in the morning, so that he could walk the twenty miles to Gunnocks and be home with good light. The entire walk was downhill and Mattie loved walking.

When Mattie and I drove to fairs, we used to leave at four or five o'clock in the morning; he drove down, while I slept. When the fair was over, I drove the two of us back to Gunnocks.

On one particular occasion, we were at the 27 March fair in Carlow. There was one man who used to attend with ten bullocks, the sort of cattle that I liked to buy. I had bid plenty for them, but he hadn't accepted my offer.

This man wore a theatrical wig, with a soft hat pulled down over it. You could tell that he was old when you looked at his face, but he had long hair hanging over his shoulders. It looked ridiculous, particularly in those days when everybody kept their hair cut tight.

'Look,' I said to Mattie. 'Stand in here on these cattle and keep looking after them and keep anybody else from getting in on them and I'll go off.'

I planned to return in a few minutes to see whether the man had changed his mind and would give me the cattle. After a few minutes I saw Mattie running up the fair, looking for me.

'What happened?'

'Ah,' he says, 'that's a horrid contrary auld fella.'

'Did you say something to him?'

'Ah, I said nothing to him, sure I only just said to him, "Isn't it a wonder you wouldn't go and get your hair cut." Then he flew off and chased me with a stick.'

'It's no wonder if you said that to him. Didn't you know well it's a wig?'

'Ah sure I did,' he said. 'But I wanted to get a rise out of him anyway.'

On another occasion in Carlow I told Mattie to go off to get his breakfast and that I would go and get mine after I had paid a few men. We arranged to meet at the car at around eleven o'clock, but he had the keys to let himself in if I showed up late.

As it happened, I got back to the car first. Assuming that there had been some kind of delay, I climbed into the car and started reading the newspaper.

At that time there used to be all kinds of stands at the fair, where they sold second-hand clothes, crockery, buckets, implements and things like that. There was a clothing stand twenty or thirty yards from the car, and when I looked up after some time I realised that the man showing off the clothes was Mattie. He had been employed by the man who owned the stand, as a model, to try on the clothes.

Then the owner would shout, 'Who'll give me ten shillings for this', or eight shillings, and then some fellow would shout out that he'd give three shillings for the article. Different items might be knocked down for four or five shillings, or might not sell at all. Anything that was knocked down was parcelled and handed to the buyer.

No matter what the article of clothing was, Mattie put it on and strutted up and down on the stand. Not only was he trying on men's clothes, he was trying on ladies' coats as well.

On another occasion we were in Nenagh and it was difficult to get a cattle truck or railway wagon for the cattle. Although the train had forty-two wagons – what was known as a 'rake' of wagons – we were near the back of the line and weren't going to get our cattle onto the first special train. Shortly after that I realised that Mattie had disappeared and I thought that he had gone for a cup of tea.

The rule was, once you put your hand on a wagon and walked along it, that meant that the wagon was reserved for you and you could load your cattle into it. Very often there would be a dispute as to who had their hand on the wagon first, but in general the system worked well.

The loading of cattle took a good while. Once the first rake of wagons was full, it had to be pulled out and taken down the line, so that the second rake of wagons could be pulled from a lay-by into the station. By the time the second rake appeared, there would be twenty or thirty people waiting to put their hand on a wagon.

I went up along to try to put a hand on a wagon, but I knew I had no hope of getting on to it. But to my surprise, who did I see, only Mattie, who had walked down the railway line, climbed up, got into one of the cattle wagons and was leaning over the door of it when it was backed into the station.

Well, I need hardly tell you, there was a queer lot of talk and abuse at him for doing such a thing, but he thoroughly enjoyed it and we got possession of the wagon. It was only somebody like Mattie who would do something like that. Mattie was exceptionally smart.

When Mattie was around seventy years old, he was carrying a bucket of water on the handlebars of his bike and he went out onto the road. The bucket struck his wheel, he overbalanced and a car came up, ran into him and killed him. Everybody was terribly sad.

13

JOE AND THE ECONOMIC WAR

The first Fianna Fáil government, which was elected in 1932, introduced economic policies that ruined the Irish cattle trade, which was the backbone of the economy at that time. Fianna Fáil was founded in 1926 by the veterans of the anti-Treaty side of the Civil War to provide an alternative to Cumann na nGaedhael. The party was led by Éamon de Valera, who was hugely popular, and advocated a return to a tillage-based agricultural economy, which would support the maximum number of people in rural Ireland.

It advocated breaking up the larger farms and distributing the land among smaller farmers and landless labourers. These land-reform measures would be accomplished by expanding the powers of the Irish Land Commission. These policies were summarised in the political slogan of the time: 'The bullock for the road; the land for the people.'

Fianna Fáil also wanted to introduce a policy of economic protectionism, to shield local industry from international competition. It was prepared to introduce protectionism despite the disastrous effect this policy had upon the live cattle export trade to England.

Finally, the party wanted to discontinue the payment of land annuities to the British government. The land annuities were the annual payments made by farmers to the British government by tenants who had purchased their holdings under the Land Acts. The Cumann na nGaedhael government had collected and paid these annuities to the British under agreements it had made in the early 1920s.

Fianna Fáil was elected to government in 1932 and informed the British government that they would no longer pay the annuities. The British responded by imposing a tariff on Irish agricultural products. The Irish retaliated to this measure by putting a tariff on coal, cement and other manufactured goods from England. While the UK was largely unaffected by the Economic War, the Irish economy was crippled.

De Valera appointed Sean Lemass as minister for industry, to encourage native industries. Lemass established the state-owned Industrial Credit Corporation to foster industry, but few viable industries were set up. One of the most successful enterprises was the Dubarry shoe factory in Ballinasloe.

The cost of the Economic War to Ireland is estimated to have been around £50 million over six years. Cattle exports to Britain fell from 750,000 in 1930 to 500,000 in 1934. The value of Irish agricultural exports fell from £36.3 million in 1931 to £17.9 million in 1934.

The price of cattle tumbled, emigration to England increased and unemployment rose sharply. In 1931, the number of unemployed people in the Irish state was 29,000. By 1933, this number had risen to 96,000, and by 1935 it was 138,000. The wages of agricultural labourers fell as low as eight shillings per week, which was barely a living wage.

After a few years, de Valera decided to come to terms with both the British and the Irish cattle industry. The 1934 Coal-Cattle Pact eased problems. In 1938, the Anglo-Irish Trade Agreement settled the land-annuities question with a once-off payment of £10 million to the United Kingdom.

I am now going to recount my experiences during the Economic War, which were quite interesting and should be recorded for posterity.

The Economic War took place in the 1930s, between the time Fianna Fáil took power and the beginning of the Second World War. I am not competent to go into the reasons for the Economic War, but I can give some background to events.

In the early 1930s, Mister de Valera – the leader of the first Fianna Fáil government – told the British government that he would retain the £3 million that Irish farmers paid annually to the British government, for land annuities. De Valera said that the money was not due to Britain and that the money should be retained in Ireland.

Negotiations went on for a while, but in July of that year, the British clapped £2 per head on every live bovine animal leaving the country, to recoup their losses from the land annuities. At that time, all animals left the country live, either going to England or to the north of Ireland.

At a later date they increased the tariff to £4, and then it increased to £6 per head. The price of cattle was very low at the time – between £15 and £16 – so it was a very serious matter to have to pay a tariff of £6.

Tariffs were also put on sheep, horses and other livestock, but I'm only interested in the cattle.

There were at least two elections over the issue, and in each case the farmers voted that the Economic War should go on. Well, the people voted for the Economic War, I think we'll put it that way. However, a large number of farmers voted that way as well, particularly in Clare and the west of Ireland.

My first experience of the Economic War took place in July of 1932. I had some nice bullocks in the Dublin cattle market, and a very decent man, a north-of-Ireland man called Paddy Cassidy, bought a pen of short-horn bullocks from me. I was very friendly with Paddy Cassidy; he was a very decent man who had a fine trade in Scotland at the time.

He told me that there was a £2 tariff on the cattle, so he would pay me £18 and I was to give him a £2 luck penny per head. He told me that if the dispute was over by the following week and the cattle got through without a tariff, then he'd give me back the £2 per head. We all assumed that the government would back down as soon as the British put on the tariff.

The value of the cattle continued to fall as the tariff rose to £6, and after a while I was buying big four-year-old bullocks for £4. Whatever price the man asked me for a bullock, I'd tell him that I'd give him one pound for every leg of him.

'Would you give me nothing for the tail?' they'd say to me. They'd hold out for a while, but eventually they'd give them to me.

I was feeding a lot of cattle at the time and was looking for the plainer sort of a bullock, that was lowish in the money. The lowest I ever got was £2 and ten shillings in Loughrea; I got plenty of them for between £3 and ten shillings and £4.

The £4 bullocks were fed in the normal way and sold for £6 or £7 in the Dublin market. By the time they arrived in England, with a £6 tariff, they sold for £12 or £13, which was no burden at the time for the English buyers.

Between the early years of the State and 1942, a great deal of public spending was controlled by the county councils. In some counties – such as County Meath – the farmers controlled the county council, which meant that they had political as well as economic power. The Local Government (Ireland) Act of 1898 had granted full democratic control of all local affairs to county and district councils. Previously, county-level services had been administered by grand juries, which had been dominated by large landowners since the seventeenth century. This Act passed the responsibilities of the grand juries to directly elected councillors. The electoral franchise was widened greatly, to include all male householders and occupiers.

The county and district councils created a political platform for proponents of Home Rule, displacing unionist grand juries. The enfranchisement of local voters helped to create a body of experienced politicians. These politicians entered national politics in Ireland in the 1920s, thereby increasing the political stability of the Irish Free State and Northern Ireland.

Under the Local Government Act of 1925, these councils were responsible for most local services, including local health, sanitation, sewerage, water, waste disposal, road construction and maintenances, defence, fire and safety, social welfare, and public assistance. It also advised the national government on local education, agricultural services, telephones and tourism. Most importantly, the county councils were responsible for local taxation, establishing the level of rates levied to maintain local services. Finally, the councils were in charge of hiring county-council employees. This often led to a significant level of patronage and corruption at local-government level.

During the War of Independence, Meath County Council was dominated by Sinn Féin. In the 1920s, the council was dominated by the pro-Treaty wing of Sinn Féin – Cumann na nGaedheal – and the Farmers' Party. Both of these parties were sympathetic to the live cattle export industry.

Fianna Fáil came to power in 1932 with a mandate for radical social and economic reform. However, Fianna Fáil's protectionist economic policies had a ruinous effect upon the live cattle export trade, a factor that turned many farmers in Meath against the new party. Other farmers turned to Fianna Fáil during this period, to take advantage of the political patronage available to Fianna Fáil supporters.

In order to export cattle to England during the 1930s, farmers needed export licences. These were distributed by the Department of Agriculture to the Meath County Council Committee of Agriculture. Farmers who needed export licenses knew that the quickest way to get them was through the local Fianna Fáil Cumann (organisation or club) in their local area.

Fianna Fáil won control of the Meath County Council in 1934, winning twenty out of the thirty-five seats. Fine Gael – an amalgam of Cumann na nGaedheal and the Farmers' Party – won the other fifteen seats. But the council was still dominated by farmers, with twelve elected for Fianna Fáil and thirteen for Fine Gael.

The English cattle trade was not doing well in the 1930s, and British farmers were quite pleased to see the tariffs on Irish cattle. In addition to the tariffs, the British government decided to impose a quota on the number of Irish cattle being imported. This quota was reduced each year and – whatever about the effect of the tariff – the quota was fatal altogether. The price of cattle was down to next to nothing and you just couldn't get rid of them.

Under the quota system, you needed a licence for every animal you exported. The regular cattle shippers got a good number of licences, which meant that they got good prices for the cattle. They certainly didn't give licences to me, or to any of the cattle feeders, but we had a few of our own because we had been sending cattle to Nelsons in Glasgow. Nelsons were very big boners and took between 1,300 and 1,400 bullocks [per week]. We had also been sending cattle to McCanns in Manchester, and the number of licences you got was based on the number of cattle you had shipped during previous years.

My father and I used to go down to the North Wall, when we were shipping cattle, to check that the animals were all right when they were being graded and loaded.

The cattle would be graded before they were loaded onto the boats, and the idea was to give them a low value for tariff purposes and then give them a high value for the purpose of the bounty. The bounty was a subsidy that the Irish government had brought in to help people to get rid of cattle. When cattle were exported or slaughtered, the owner was entitled to a bounty.

There was a grader at the North Wall, whose job it was to value the cattle. It was his job to know the price of the cattle, so that you wouldn't put too high a value on them, since the higher the price, the higher the bounty.

I had some very big bullocks on this particular day, which I had bought in Athenry for £6. When I was going home on the train, men were saying to me, 'What will you do with them? Will you hang them around your neck or what will you do with them? You'll never get to sell those cattle.'

When it came to the back end of the year, they were very fine bullocks, perhaps twelve-and-a-half- or thirteen-hundredweight. It just so happened that the grader was on holiday or was sick and that his job was being carried out by vets from the Department of Agriculture.

A vet called McCarthy – whom I knew – came to me and said, 'Look, aren't those big bullocks in that pen belonging to you?'

'They are,' I said.

'Look,' he said. 'I haven't an idea what those cattle are worth, what are you valuing them at?'

'I'm valuing them at £13 each.'

'That's fair enough,' he said. 'We'll pay you the £4 bounty.'

He was quite satisfied with that and I needn't tell you that I was too, because I had them valued at £9 for tariff purposes.

So the animals cost £6; were valued for tariff at £9; and were valued for bounty at £13. That gives you an idea of the complicated business that went on during the Economic War.

Men used to buy these export licences; there was nothing illegal or dishonest about it. The men who lived in the north of Ireland or along the border used to have them and brought them down to the Dublin market. They'd ask £4 for them; I'd give £3 or £3 ten shillings for them, because I wanted to get rid of the cattle and get good price for them. My cousin Joe could never understand how I got the licences. I bought them from these men and they knew that I'd give them a bit more than other people.

Sometimes – but not often – I'd bid for licences when I was buying cattle in the west. I'd offer £4 for the cattle and the man would ask me how much I'd give him if there were licences going with the cattle. I'd pay him for the animal and for the licences, which could then be transferred onto any beast you liked.

Certain people got the licences, perhaps because of political reasons. There was a local herd beside us who had the grass of a heifer as part of his wages – he was entitled to put his heifer into a field for free grazing. He came to me and he said, 'I have a roan short-horn heifer, she's about a year and a half old. Would you buy her from me?'

Now he was a very decent man, but he knew quite well that I wouldn't be interested in young heifers, and he said immediately to me, 'I'll give you two licences with the heifer.'

Well, he possibly – and I only say possibly – may have been legally allowed to have one licence for her, but certainly not two. I went over and

I bought the heifer from him. To the best of my memory I gave him £3 for her and he gave me two licences with her, and I calculated them at £3 each, so that I gave him £9 for his heifer.

As I say, he had no right to have two licences but that was his business. When I had her bought, he said to me, 'Sure you may as well leave her here, because I have the grass on this man's land for the year and there was always the chance that I could get one or two more licences for her.'

I remember by the end of the year, he had collected six licences for the one heifer. Of course, he shouldn't have. The state, or whoever was in charge, had no right to give him those. Anyway, he got them and good luck to him, because there was no more decent man in the place.

Because the west of Ireland had no dairying – it was all dry cattle – the government decided to build a sugar factory in Tuam, to encourage people to grow beet. I thought that it was a crazy idea, because they were not used to that; in some of the parishes down there, there wasn't a single plough, and they weren't interested.

There were already sugar factories in Carlow and Thurles; if they'd built one in Wexford, then that would have been grand, but they weren't the right politics in Wexford. In the west of Ireland – Clare, Mayo, Galway, Connemara – they were all de Valera people.

There were a lot of farmers opposed to it, because they were required to grow beet to keep the factory going. On the other hand, a lot of labouring men were in favour of it because it would give employment.

I remember a bitter row in Athenry at around six in the morning. I was buying cattle by the archway and the cattle were packed tight. It was a big fair and you'd be shoving to get through the cattle. There was even a danger you would be stood on.

People used to put boards across the windows of their houses to stop the horns from breaking the glass, and the cattle were pressed up against the door of the houses.

I remember a man standing at the door of his house in just a shirt and trousers, having a row with two or three farmers outside who were opposed to the starting of the beet factory in Tuam. This man – being a labouring man – was all in favour of it, and they were hammer and tongs against each other. The man in the house was outnumbered by the farmers, who were out in the street trying to sell their cattle.

I remember that the farmers were all pulling me, saying, 'Here Mister Ward, would you buy this one?'

It was amusing to see this man who'd been sleeping in his shirt, holding up his trousers with both hands in the middle of a row with the farmers.

I used to go to Galway for my holidays, with my father. I'd drive off in the car and, when I got out into the country, I'd get out and walk around, looking at the cattle as I went along.

There's a big quarry somewhere outside Galway, and I remember seeing a very big short-horn bullock in it. I suppose you could say that he was being fed in the quarry, but in fact he was just being starved in it. He was just existing in the quarry.

It so happened that I saw the same bullock in the fair in Eyre Square. He was a huge beast, as big as a horse, but very badly made. He was a tall leggy short-horn bullock, but he wasn't worth more than £4 or £4 ten shillings.

I went up to the man and asked him the price of the bullock. I bid £5 and he took it.

'Was that bullock bred in a quarry?' I asked him.

'He was,' he said. 'How did you know that?'

'Well,' I said, 'I saw him there, a couple of years ago.'

'You're perfectly right,' he said. 'I gave £9 for that bullock four years ago and I just couldn't keep him, so I left him in the quarry.'

I was able to get a licence for the bullock and was able to ship him, but he was a very bad thriver, after three or four years of starvation in the quarry.

When cattle were so cheap, land was also worth nothing. People simply wouldn't buy land, because if they bought cattle to put on it, they worried that they mightn't be able to sell them. They also had no money to buy cattle, because the ones that were selling cattle had made nothing from them and couldn't go out to buy more. People would try to save the money instead.

Johnny O'Connor and his father, who were from Dingle, used to put an advertisement in the paper that they wanted three thousand acres of good grazing land in either Meath, Kildare or Dublin. They would be offered up to ten thousand acres, so they could choose the land they wanted. The O'Connors were very prominent Fianna Fáil men and they were helped, I would say, in a lot of ways. They were probably entitled to a lot of export licences.

They were an asset to the people of Dingle, who had been unable to sell their bullocks. When the O'Connors had a trainload of cattle, they loaded them in Tralee and shipped them to Meath and Kildare. The cattle were small, so were able to put eleven into each wagon and had forty-two wagons on each train.

They were unloaded in Hazelhatch, where they were rested for three or four days. Then they walked them to the land that they rented around Dunshaughlin, Navan and all over north County Dublin.

The O'Connors had rented around six acres of land from my Aunt Ita at Nuttstown. The herd told me that in the first six weeks that they had it, 1,600 cattle passed through that land.

During the Economic War, a different type of north-of-Ireland man came down to the Dublin cattle market. These were farmers and small dealers who lived quite close to either side of the border.

Because of the tariffs and the quota, if they could buy an animal down here for £4 and could smuggle it across the border, they got £6 for it on the far side, or maybe even more.

I used to cater for these smugglers in the Dublin cattle markets; they would specifically ask me to bring in a certain number of black cattle the following week. The cattle were smuggled at night-time, and these men would not buy a Hereford bullock from you because he had a white face. Neither would they buy a white bullock – or a red one – because they were more likely to be seen at night.

There were other smugglers who would tell me to bring a certain number of red cattle the following week. These would be men who owned land along the border. They kept a certain number of red cattle in a field, and the customs men would check each week to make sure that they hadn't been moved across the border. That's why these farmers wanted the same number of red cattle each week, to make up the numbers on the south side of the border, so that the custom officials would think that they were the same cattle.

One of the reasons why they would deal with me was because all of my cattle were my own; I wasn't an agent for sellers who might ask questions. They also knew that I was unlikely to talk, because I knew the men involved and I knew that the cattle were being smuggled.

In other cases the border went through a man's farm, so the animals crossed the border by walking the length of a field. I was friendly with one such man – by the name of Barber – whose house was divided by the border. The kitchen was on one side of the border and the front of the house was on the other. He was a Protestant and was great friends with Arthur Jackson, who lived near Gunnocks. When Barber wanted cattle, he often bought them from me. He was more into the horse business: he preferred to be smuggling horses rather than cattle.

The customs officials were in on it and I know that there were very high government ministers involved in the smuggling business too. One of the biggest smugglers was Sir Basil Brooke, the premier of Northern Ireland. He lived at Brookborough, and it was very easy to drive cattle across the river into the Brookborough demesne at Aughnacloy, where the river is shallow. He didn't buy the cattle himself; they were bought by Captain King, who took them across for him.

As stand-holders in the Dublin cattle market, we knew perfectly well that these cattle were being smuggled. The smaller men used to pay for them with big rolls of north-of-Ireland notes, while men like Captain King paid with a cheque.

One year, I went to the October fair in Galway and saw two magnificent roan bullocks standing in the middle of Eyre Square. I paid £6 for them, and the man who sold them told me that they were fed in the grounds of University College Galway.

I was at the fair in Tuam on one occasion during the Economic War. There are only two hotels in Tuam. The first was McHughs, which I never stayed in, and the other was the Imperial, which was run by Mrs Guy and she ran it with a rod of steel.

The problem with Guys was that it was alright if there were six or twelve people staying there, but during the fair there could be one hundred people staying there. They also used to say – I don't know if it's true or not – that they never took the clothes off the bed, they left them there from one end of the year to the other, so they'd be fairly damp. You slept with your clothes on in any of these places, as well as sleeping between the blankets.

At the October fair in Tuam, there would be between ten and twelve thousand cattle on the green, across an area of around ten acres, and they'd all be red. At any rate, ninety percent would be red and the balance would be roans and some whites. There would be nothing else, no white-heads and no blacks. They'd be grand cattle, all with horns. They branded their cattle with tar brands and forty percent of them would be branded with a H.

I went up to James Hession, who was from Roundfort. He was a very heavy drinker and had evidently been drinking all night and was in a very rough humour. He had twenty of the loveliest red bullocks I ever bought in my life, there wasn't a scrap of white on them and I would say they had a common father. They had beautiful, tapering horns on them and they were all dark red.

Cattle were worth very little at the time and I got the twenty bullocks for £8 each. That was a good enough price for them, but they were outstandingly good cattle.

Hession and his son were there with the cattle. The son – who had no say whatsoever – was a nice, very delicate chap. The father put up to be high class, but he was a pig-rough jumping bowsie of a man. He insisted that I write on the ticket that I bought eight bullocks at £20 apiece. It came to the same amount, but he was able to go around the fair saying 'Oh, look what I got for my cattle, you're all selling your cattle too cheap, I got £20 apiece'.

When the cattle were loaded, I met him in Guys hotel, where he had consumed a lot more drink. He was in a contrary mood and he refused to give me a luck penny. Undoubtedly he lost a lot of money on the cattle, because he'd have fed them for some time, which would have cost him. However, that wasn't my fault

I was very annoyed, because it was considered very much as a slight to not give a luck penny. I was regarded – and it's no harm to say it – as a very decent man and I never kicked on anybody.

A number of people were around at the time, including Peter and Ulick McDonald and the Moyletts and they saw this going on. I wouldn't get into a row with a man in that condition, but Hession got very annoyed, lifted up a chair and pegged it through the stained glass window of the Imperial hotel, smashing it.

Mrs Guy came in told me that we'd have to pay for it. Hession bust his way out and I had to pay for the window. After the father was gone, the son told me that it was all a great shame and that I was entitled to two shillings a head for those twenty cattle.

'Oh, look,' he said. 'When he sobers up, after maybe a week, he'll send it to you.'

I never got it and I never dealt with him again. I was always like that, if a person did me a bad turn, I never went back near him. They knew the kind of beast I'd buy and they'd know I was a good buyer, so they'd get somebody else to sell the beast for them. I'd have been fairly quick and I'd have seen them beforehand with the cattle.

'Hey Mister Ward,' a fellow would say to me. 'You'll buy them.'

'Ach,' I'd say. 'I'll have a look at them.'

'Ah no,' I'd say then. 'They're not just what I want.'

But I'd know darn well that they belonged to somebody else.

Both Laurence of Fieldstown and myself were great friends with Ulick and Peter McDonald, two brothers who were also from Roundfort. Peter had around seven hundred acres of land at Roundfort and he fed a lot of cattle. The Land Commission took a lot of that land from him and didn't give him any land to replace it. He used to take land in County Meath; I used to buy cattle for him and sometimes I used to give him a hand to sell them.

I remember him saying that we thought that we had great land in County Meath, but that the best land he had ever fed cattle on was in a place called Rynana in County Limerick; it was marvellous land.

'I never saw cattle thrive like them,' he said. 'You couldn't keep the grass down on that place.'

Shannon Airport is built on Rynana, but I suppose that the name is still on the townland maps, it's an awful pity that they turned it into a concrete jungle.

Peter also used to take a lot of land near Claremorris, which was low-lying bog land. He used to get it cheap, because any local cattle that were put on that land got sick and died. Peter would buy cattle in Clifden and put them on the land in Claremorris. For whatever reason, none of his cattle ever got sick and died on that land.

Peter and Ulick used to show around sixty bullocks at the Tuam fair, which would have been bought down in Clifden and that country. Some of them would have been pollys – good ones – but they would be the only blacks on show, apart from a few shown by a man called Joyce, who also had land in Connemara. Both Laurence of Fieldstown and myself would often buy twenty cattle from Peter.

Peter had a mongrel collie, who was the best cattle dog that I have ever seen. He'd have him there in the green, with cattle milling all around, but he'd never get stood on or kicked. The dog would herd cattle for you and if one of them ran away, the dog would be after the beast, he'd bit the heels off him and get him back. Of course, it was dangerous; he could have jumped the bullock on top of anybody who happened to be in the way.

I remember the big railway loading bank at Tuam. It was about a quarter of a mile in length and you loaded cattle on both sides of the track. There were two or three hundred men hitting the cattle with ash plants, to get them into a wagon. You'd often get a belt of a stick by accident when a fellow would raise it up to hit a bullock and he'd bring it back too far and hit you on the head with it.

Sometimes a bullock would get mixed with somebody else's and Peter's dog would follow him up and get him back to you. He'd go to any length; he'd bite the bullock through six or eight lots of cattle and he'd have him back at the wagon in no time.

Towards the end of the Economic War, cattle began to get a bit dearer. I gave ten guineas for some really magnificent bullocks in Tuam, to a man called McHugh. They were very big bullocks, four or five years old. When I was paying him, he started to cry and told me that they had cost £14 two years before. I must say that I was very upset about it; however, I did deal with him again afterwards.

Old cows were worth very little, because the same tariff went on old cows as went onto the bullocks. If the tariff was £6 and the cow was only worth £5, then you simply couldn't sell them. A lot of people used to stray their cows; they'd just leave them in the mountains or the bogs. In other cases, they were brought to the fairs, and if they couldn't get a few shillings for them, then they just left them behind and went home. Nobody would bother stealing them, because they weren't worth anything.

I remember looking at an enormous red cow in Athenry and a man asked me whether I'd ever seen such a big cow in my life. She was being sold for two shillings and sixpence.

The buyer paid over the two and sixpence and the seller handed it straight back to him.

'What's that?' he asked.

'That's the luck penny,' the seller said.

'I didn't expect that at all,' he said.

'Maybe you didn't, but I never gave less than half a crown for luck in my life and I'm not going to give less now,' he said.

The old cows and the skinny cows that came out of the west of Ireland and Kerry weren't worth anything at all. Farmers just strayed them; letting them live on the mountains.

Con Crowley, his brother Gerry, and a German named Wezenfeld decided that they would build a meat factory in Roscrea, County Tipperary, to process these old cows; this was the first meat factory in Ireland.

These old cows were put into tins for export, which meant that they avoided any tariff or duty. They sent men out to buy cows from all over the country. They bought thousands of them; it was a great credit to the Crowley family. The Crowleys were great de Valera people and they got every help going to do what they did.

The factory didn't affect me, because I didn't keep cows, but I used to see hundreds of them being put together in the fairs in the west. Sometimes whole trainloads of them would be sent up, after they had been lying on a mountain for years. Some of them were fourteen or fifteen years old and were so weak that it was hard to get them to walk into the wagon, so they had to lift them in. After a few years they had got rid of all the old cows, but the Crowleys kept the factory going until some years ago, when the family sold it.

De Valera's government wanted to reduce the number of cattle in the country as far as possible, so they gave a bounty of £2 to anybody who would kill a calf rather than rear it. Irish people in general would not like to kill something like that, even for the sake of getting £2. They'd rather stray it, anything you like, but they didn't want to kill it.

A number of people had no money, so they killed the calves and threw them into a quarry, or threw them to the greyhounds, or threw them over a cliff. They didn't want the bother of burying them. It was a horrible thing to happen and we can look back on it now with sorrow.

And that's that.

There's one more thing. Joseph Connolly, one of the Fianna Fáil ministers, said in a speech that I remember well, that the Irish cattle trade is dead and dead for ever. If he was alive now, he would have to eat his words and they wouldn't be too sweet either, when you look at the number of cattle that are being exported at present.

In the 1930s, Fianna Fáil introduced a series of land-reform measures, to break up big farms in Meath and Kildare and to distribute the land to small farmers from the west of Ireland. The system was administered by the Irish Land Commission.

As mentioned earlier, the Irish Land Commission was originally set up under Gladstone in 1870, to adjudicate in landlord-tenant disputes and to administer the 'Three Fs' of fair rent, fixity of tenure and freedom of sale for the tenant. It was also pivotally involved in the sale of the landlord's estates at the turn of the twentieth century.

The powers of the Land Commission were increased after the foundation of the Irish Free State in 1922. The Land Commission was empowered to compulsorily purchase farms which weren't being used, or which were on long-term leases. These farms were subdivided and sold to other farmers, whose existing holdings weren't viable.

The people whose farms were subdivided weren't paid in cash, but with government bonds, which provided a small income to the recipients, but which had a negligible capital value. The new landowners paid cash annuities to the Irish government.

Under Senator Joseph Connolly —who was the Minister for Lands and Fisheries between 1933 and 1936 — a number of farming families from the western seaboard were resettled on large compulsorily acquired cattle farms in Leinster and Munster. Connolly oversaw the establishment of the Meath Gaeltachts in Rath Cairn and Gibbstown, with small farmers from Connemara, Donegal, Mayo and Kerry.

Under the terms of the migration schemes, farmers surrendered their holdings in the Gaeltacht in exchange for larger, more fertile farms in County Meath. The settlers were expected to demonstrate the superiority of tillage farming to the locals, who were mostly involved in drystock and dairying. However, after the Second World War, the Gaeltacht farmers also switched to dairying and drystock. These colonies also bore the expectation that they would gradually convert the local population to the language and lifestyle of small Gaeltacht farmers.

14

LAURENCE OF FIELDSTOWN

GOES TO DONCASTER

Laurence Ward of Fieldstown was my father's second cousin. He lived with his sisters, Anna, Frances, Bridgit and Sarah in north County Dublin. He used to travel to fairs with my father and myself. He and I were very close.

Laurence of Fieldstown used to go to Doncaster, South Yorkshire, frequently, where he was well known and well liked by the breeders at the bloodstock sales. As a younger man, he used to hunt and ride in point-to-point races. He took a great interest in breeding horses and had his own colours. Over the years he had bred quite a number of good horses, notably The Swift and The Swiftfoot, and used to sell yearlings at the sales in Doncaster.

Lilla and I were in Fieldstown one evening, shortly after the war, when we met Laurence on his way to Doncaster to see the Saint Leger and to sell yearlings in the sale. He was all dressed up and ready for his grand-nephew to drive him to the boat.

Laurence assumed that things in England wouldn't have changed over the course of the war. He was certainly surprised by what he found. After his trip, he told us that he was either on the brink of starvation, or in the lap of luxury.

He got nothing to eat on the boat or on the train, and it was nearly eleven o'clock by the time the train arrived in Peterborough. He thought that he would be allowed to sleep in the carriage and continue to Doncaster in the morning, but the guard simply told him to get out of the train.

Because the train wasn't leaving for Doncaster until six o'clock the following morning, Laurence wondered about getting a place to stop for the night. He approached a policeman who was standing on the platform. The policeman pointed out a row of houses. My uncle, as I always called him, could barely see them because it was dark and the blackout was still in force in England at the time.

'Start knocking on the door of the first house and see if they let you in,' the policeman said. 'If not, move on to the next house and then work your way down one side of the street and up the other side.'

After three or four houses, a woman opened the door and Laurence asked her for a bed for the night.

She said to him, 'Do you have a pound on you?'

'I have,' he said.

'Give it to me,' she said.

'Oh, I want to be called in the morning and I want my breakfast,' he said.

She told him that there would be no call and no breakfast. Then she told him to go up to the top of the stairs, where he would find a big room with a bed in it.

There were eight or ten men there before him, so he went around touching the beds, until he finally found one that was empty. He got into it and fell asleep.

When he awoke the next morning, he found that there was no business of getting washed or anything like that. He was glad it was dark when he found a bed, because if he had known how filthy dirty it was, then he wouldn't have stayed in it.

Then he made his way out to the train station and continued on to Doncaster, where there happened to be five other men, four of whom were playing cards together. In those days, men used to play cards on the train, travelling to and from fairs. There would usually be four men who knew each other quite well and who were very interested in cards. They got into the same carriage and spread a rug or an overcoat across their knees. They played the cards into the centre of the coats and kept the money on the windowsill of the carriage.

Personally, I didn't care for cards and I wasn't very good at them anyway. However, Laurence of Fieldstown was very fond of three particular games – spoiled five, twenty-five and solo.

Four of the men in Laurence's carriage that day were professional card players, who were known as 'card sharpers'. They played for high stakes and weren't terribly honest. A person who played with them without knowing the game very well could get very badly stung.

Laurence took a huge interest in their game and counted £150 in the kitty. After some time, one of them said that he had had enough, that he had no more money left. Another one of them turned to Laurence and asked him whether he'd like to take a hand.

'Ah no,' said Laurence, 'I wouldn't be interested. I was just interested in looking at it.'

Then they turned to the other man who was sitting there reading a book and asked him whether he would like to take a hand.

'Well, yes,' he said. 'But I don't know very much about them, would you explain the game to me? We'll play one round to get me in on it and then I'll play with you.'

Of course, that was exactly the type of man that the sharpers wanted: somebody who knew nothing about the game. They played a couple of hands to show him how to play. He then started to play with the three other men and played very well. Laurence calculated that there was £300 in notes in the kitty.

After a short while, one of the original players threw his cards into the kitty and said that he had had enough of it. Then the other two threw in their hands and the man with the book cleared out the kitty. Of course, the man with the book was a bigger card-sharp than the other four, but they didn't know him.

When Laurence got to Doncaster, he sold his yearlings and lodged with the same people that he always lodged with. They happened to be undertakers and took in a few lodgers over their premises.

He was welcomed by any number of people who hadn't seen him for years. These were English people and Irish people and Irish men who lived in England but who had bought cattle from him in the Dublin market. He then attended the breeders' dinner, where he was toasted by the other breeders, because he had been absent for the course of the war.

Laurence made particular mention of meeting the two brothers Molloy, from Bohulla in County Mayo. As young men, they were two of a large number of men who travelled from Mayo to England every year, for seasonal work on farms.

Mr Doyle, the stationmaster of Balla station in the early years of the century, told me a story about these seasonal workers. Every year, at a certain time, word would come to Balla that the harvest was ready for them in England. Hundreds of men from Kilogues, Ballyvary, Foxford and Knock all came to Balla to get the train to Dublin, so that they could take the boat to England.

These men assumed that a special train would be arranged to bring them to Dublin, but it wouldn't have been possible to arrange a special train so quickly. Instead, the railway used to get a rake of cattle wagons, wash them out and make seats out of wooden boards nailed across the floors. The men went into these wagons and were quite happy to sit in them until the train reached Dublin.

The problem was that they often sat in Balla for several hours, or maybe even a whole day. Because they didn't have anything to do and didn't have anything to eat, they took a lot of drink.

When they were drunk, they wouldn't stay seated on the train, they would get up on top of the wagons, not realising the danger of the bridges. The bridges would hit them on the head and knock them back into the cattle wagon or knock them off the train.

On one occasion there was a very bad accident in Balla. The road leading from the town to the railway station was dead straight for nearly half a mile. When the men in the town heard the train whistle, they assumed that their train was arriving. They thought that they'd miss their train if they didn't get down there quickly. They ran like billy-o down to the train, with drink taken.

The people at the front of the group ran onto the platform and realised that it was an oncoming train and wasn't for them at all. But the ones behind couldn't see this and the ones in front were shoved out onto the lines and several of them were killed.

The two brothers Molloy were good customers of both Laurence and myself. They had travelled to England as potato pickers as young men. After a while, they started buying land in England and planting the potatoes themselves. During the war – when it was impossible to get labour in England – they were able to draw huge numbers of men from County Mayo to pick the potatoes. In those days potatoes had to be picked by hand, because there was no machinery.

The two brothers Molloy would have made a tremendous amount of money out of the potato trade, as well as keeping cattle and several hundred acres of corn. I don't know exactly how much land they had, but I know that after the war they had several thousands of acres.

They bought land between Harrowgate and Doncaster, laid it down in grass and brought huge numbers of Irish cattle to England. They had one brother who lived on the family farm in Mayo, and he would send them cattle, but in general they bought cattle in Dublin.

During his last trip to Doncaster, a number of years after the war, Laurence suffered a heart attack. Miss Keogh's people called to say that he wasn't well and that his nephews did not have passports. Mis Keogh was a trained nurse who came to Fieldstown for a week to look after one of the four sisters, broke her leg falling over the terrier, and ended up staying for twenty years. Because my passport was in order, I was able to leave that evening for the boat at the North Wall. I took the train as far as Crewe, where I was told by a porter that the train wouldn't be leaving until six in the morning. I told him where I was going and gave him a tip. He opened a carriage door and let me into the train. I don't know if I slept, but I certainly rested for the night.

I had never been to Doncaster before and didn't know anybody in that part of England. They gave me quite a reasonable breakfast in the canteen on the platform of Doncaster railway station. When I say 'reasonable', I mean that they had a bit of butter on the bread, which was unusual. They had no bacon or eggs or anything like that, although you could get a few mushrooms if you wanted them. You could have either tea or coffee and you could get cakes. Then I walked down the street to a hotel and booked in.

When I arrived in to Laurence of Fieldstown, his helper Mickey Brien was with him, reading out the prayers for the dying. Then Mickey Brien read out the racing news to him and he said that he felt much better. Laurence travelled back to Ireland and lived for a number of months.

Back in the 1840s, the Wards used to import 'pink eyes' potatoes from north Wales. They were a main-crop breed and resembled the breed known as 'lumpers'. They were immune to wart disease and were tolerant to virus diseases.

The Wards of Fieldstown East claimed that, during the Famine, their pink-eye potatoes did not take the blight on their 150-acre farm at Leestown, Co Dublin. This farm was a long, high ridge of land, with an avenue running the whole length of the farm. The land on each side of the avenue measured exactly seventy-five acres, to a yard. In the 1940s, the Irish Land Commission took over this farm – very much against the will of the Fieldstown Wards.

'They might have left it with us for a few more years till we died,' Laurence and his sister, Sarah, said to me. 'Our grandfather kept half of north County Dublin alive with the potatoes off Leestown.'

For the record, I wish to state the following fact. On the morning that Laurence of Fieldstown died, he had Miss Kehoe – his housekeeper – ring me up to come and see him at once.

'Mister Laurence says that he is going to die,' she said. Miss Kehoe was also a trained nurse, so I asked her how he was.

'He is just the same as any other day,' she said.

My wife and I drove over and went up to his room. He was sitting up in bed and threw his chequebook over to me.

'Fill that out for the Ballinasloe cattle and I will sign it,' he said.

I handed it back to him to sign, which he did. I had bought cattle at Ballinasloe for Laurence. I was not anxious to fill out the cheque but Laurence insisted. He did not want to die owing anybody money.

'Say the prayers for the dying and let me go out of this,' he said. 'I am waiting for you here all day so that I could go.'

He said the prayer with the family and died just as they finished.

POSTSCRIPT

In 1938, Joe married Lilla Doyle, the daughter of a Limerick solicitor, James A Doyle. Lilla was the great-great-granddaughter of Daniel O'Connell and also of Daniel Doyle, a prominent member of the Young Irelander movement of 1848.

Joe continued to go to fairs and to sell in the Dublin cattle markets, until these died out gradually in the decades after the Second World War. They were replaced by regional cattle marts and meat factories. Most of the railways were closed down during the 1950s and were replaced by road transport.

Joe and Lilla lived in Gunnocks until Joe's death in 2000. They had four children: Mary, Laurence, Olivia and Chris. Mary lives in Melbourne, Australia and has four children. Laurence farms in south County Meath and is married with four children. Olivia worked as a lecturer in German languages and studies at the Galway Mayo Institute of Technology. Chris works as a genealogist and researcher, and caregiver to her mother. She is the author of *The Famine in Fingal* and an upcoming book of her mother's memoirs.

The area around Gunnocks – particularly the towns of Dunboyne, Clonee and Ratoath – has become one of the fastest-growing residential and industrial areas in Ireland.